I0434791

Report to Congress on

Supporting Organizations and Donor Advised Funds

Department of the Treasury

December 2011

DEPARTMENT OF THE TREASURY
WASHINGTON, D.C. 20220

December 5, 2011

The Honorable Max Baucus
Chairman, Committee on Finance
United States Senate
Washington, DC 20510

Dear Chairman Baucus:

As mandated by section 1226(a) of the Pension Protection Act of 2006 (the PPA), the Department of the Treasury has conducted a study on the organization and operation of supporting organizations and donor advised funds. Section 1226(b) of the PPA directs the Secretary of the Treasury to submit a report on the supporting organization and donor advised fund study to Congress.

Enclosed is our report on Supporting Organizations and Donor Advised Funds. An identical letter is addressed to Senator Hatch.

Sincerely,

Emily S. McMahon
Acting Assistant Secretary (Tax Policy)

Enclosure

DEPARTMENT OF THE TREASURY
WASHINGTON, D.C. 20220

December 5, 2011

The Honorable Orrin G. Hatch
Ranking Member, Committee on Finance
United States Senate
Washington, DC 20510

Dear Senator Hatch:

As mandated by section 1226(a) of the Pension Protection Act of 2006 (the PPA), the Department of the Treasury has conducted a study on the organization and operation of supporting organizations and donor advised funds. Section 1226(b) of the PPA directs the Secretary of the Treasury to submit a report on the supporting organization and donor advised fund study to Congress.

Enclosed is our report on Supporting Organizations and Donor Advised Funds. An identical letter is addressed to Senator Baucus.

Sincerely,

Emily S. McMahon
Acting Assistant Secretary (Tax Policy)

Enclosure

December 5, 2011

The Honorable Dave Camp
Chairman, Committee on Ways and Means
U.S. House of Representatives
Washington, DC 20515

Dear Chairman Camp:

As mandated by section 1226(a) of the Pension Protection Act of 2006 (the PPA), the Department of the Treasury has conducted a study on the organization and operation of supporting organizations and donor advised funds. Section 1226(b) of the PPA directs the Secretary of the Treasury to submit a report on the supporting organization and donor advised fund study to Congress.

Enclosed is our report on Supporting Organizations and Donor Advised Funds. An identical letter is addressed to Representative Sander Levin.

Sincerely,

Emily S. McMahon
Acting Assistant Secretary (Tax Policy)

Enclosure

December 5, 2011

The Honorable Sander Levin
Ranking Member, Committee on Ways and Means
U.S. House of Representatives
Washington, DC 20515

Dear Representative Levin:

As mandated by section 1226(a) of the Pension Protection Act of 2006 (the PPA), the Department of the Treasury has conducted a study on the organization and operation of supporting organizations and donor advised funds. Section 1226(b) of the PPA directs the Secretary of the Treasury to submit a report on the supporting organization and donor advised fund study to Congress.

Enclosed is our report on Supporting Organizations and Donor Advised Funds. An identical letter is addressed to Representative Dave Camp.

Sincerely,

Emily S. McMahon
Acting Assistant Secretary (Tax Policy)

Enclosure

Table of Contents

Chapter 1: Introduction and Summary 1

Mandate and Scope of the Study 1

Executive Summary and Major Findings 5

Chapter 2: Description of Federal Tax Law Treatment of Charities, Supporting Organizations, and Donor Advised Funds 9

Public Charities vs. Private Foundations 11

SOs 20

DAFs 21

PPA Changes 22

Changes to the Law Governing SOs 23

Changes to the Law Governing DAF Sponsoring Organizations 25

Regulatory Guidance 27

Chapter 3: Empirical Description and Analysis of SOs and DAFs 28

Public Charities and Private Foundations 28

SOs 32

DAFs 44

DAF Account Requirements at Commercial NDAFs 62

Conclusions 63

Chapter 4: Public Comments on SOs and DAFs 65

General Comments about SOs 66

General Comments about DAFs 67

Donor Advice and Control 68

Charitable Contribution Deduction 69

Distribution Requirements 71

Payout Requirement for SOs 72

Payout Requirement for Non-functionally Integrated Type III SOs 73

Payout Requirement for DAFs 73

Distribution Requirements and Perpetual Existence 74

Expected Effects of the PPA 75

Effects on SOs 75

Effects on DAFs 76

Proposals from Respondents 77

Chapter 5: Answering Congressional Questions 79

Charitable Contribution Deduction 80

Distribution Requirements 81

Other Forms of Charity 82

Conclusion 83

Appendix A: Selected Bibliography 84

Appendix B: Congressional Mandate 88

Appendix C: Data Appendix 89

Appendix D: Notice 2006-109 92

Appendix E: Notice 2007-21 104

Tables

Table 2.1: Summary of Major Distinctions among Private Foundations, Public Charities, SOs, and DAF Sponsoring Organizations Post-PPA 16

Table 3.1: Public Charity and Private Foundation Information Returns, and Exempt Organization Business Income Tax Returns, Selected Financial Data, 1985-2006 30

Table 3.2: Supporting Organizations, by Type, 2006 33

Table 3.3: Supporting Organizations, by Sector, 2006 38

Table 3.4: Reported Support and Related Activities of Supported Organizations, 2006 42

Table 3.5: DAF Sponsoring Organizations by Sector, 2006 47

Table 3.6: Education Sector DAF Sponsoring Organizations, 2006 53

Table 3.7: Distribution of Aggregate DAF Values and Payout Rates of DAF Sponsoring Organizations, 2006 56

Table 3.8: Non-cash Property Donations to DAF Sponsoring Organizations, by Type of Property and Type of DAF Sponsoring Organization, 2005 61

Table 4.1: Public Comments to Notice 2007-21, by Type of Respondent...66

Table C.1: Original Reported and Adjusted Values of DAF Information, Unweighted, 2006...................91

Figures

Figure 2.1: Types of Section 501(c)(3) Organizations...10

Figure 2.2: Donor's Tradeoffs between Establishing or Contributing to a Public Charity versus a Private Foundation 14

Chapter 1: Introduction and Summary

Mandate and Scope of the Study

Title XII of the Pension Protection Act of 2006, Pub. L. 109-280, 120 Stat. 780 (2006) (the PPA) made numerous changes to provisions of the Internal Revenue Code (the Code) addressing charitable giving and tax-exempt organizations.[1] Particular changes to the law were made regarding supporting organizations (SOs) and charitable giving arrangements commonly referred to as donor advised funds (DAFs). The legislation provided a statutory definition of the term "donor advised fund" and modified the statutory definition of "supporting organization." Section 1226 of the PPA directs the Secretary of the Treasury to undertake a study on the organization and operation of SOs and DAFs and submit the findings to Congress. This report provides the results of Treasury's analysis of SOs and DAFs and responds to the questions posed by Congress.

Tax-exempt charitable organizations perform a wide variety of activities, including providing food, clothing, shelter, and other services to the needy; providing religious services; and maintaining research, educational, and cultural institutions. Others engage in indirect charitable activities, including providing support and grants to other charitable institutions. DAFs and many SOs engage in this latter type of charitable activity. In recent years, they have become increasingly relevant in the charitable sector, in terms of both their numbers and their assets.

The Code first defined an SO in 1969, and the PPA modified this definition. An SO is a public charity that supports another closely related public charity—the supported organization. Support may take the form of monetary payments or direct services to the supported organization, or charitable activity that furthers the charitable purpose of the supported organization. The SO derives its public charity status *through its relationship* with its supported organization and is therefore not required to qualify separately as a public charity, e.g., by meeting a public support test. An organization may be an SO to more than one supported organization.

The relationship between the SO and its supported organization may be very close, e.g., board members of the supported organization may control the board of the SO, or more distant. Based on the type of relationship between the SO and its supported organization, the SO is categorized as a Type I, Type II, or Type III SO. (See the discussion below.) Familiar examples of SOs include university alumni associations that conduct activities promoting the alma mater and organizations that serve as the "parent organization" in non-profit hospital systems.

The PPA added the first statutory definition of the term "donor advised fund" to the Code, although this form of charitable giving arrangement has existed for more than 70 years. The Code now defines a DAF as a fund or account at a qualified public charity—referred to in the law as the "sponsoring organization" of the DAF—over which a donor or a donor-appointed advisor retains advisory privileges regarding the investment and/or distribution of assets in the

---

[1] The text of the Act is available at http://frwebgate.access.gpo.gov/cgi-bin/getdoc.cgi?dbname=109_cong_public_laws&docid=f:publ280.109.pdf. (Last accessed December 1, 2011.)

account; thus the name "donor advised fund."[2] The sponsoring organization generally heeds the recommendations from the donor but is not compelled to do so.

In common parlance, the acronym "DAF" is sometimes used interchangeably to describe both an individual donor account maintained by the sponsoring organization and the aggregate collection of donor accounts at that sponsoring organization. In some cases where the sponsoring organization does not engage in other charitable activities beyond the management of DAFs, the acronym "DAF" has even been used to describe the sponsoring organization itself. In this report, the term "DAF" refers to the individual donor-advised account consisting of the donor's (or donors') contributions and any returns on those contributions credited to the account. For expository purposes, in this report the term "Aggregate DAF" refers to the aggregate collection of the DAFs maintained by a single sponsoring organization, which are subject to the rules and procedures established by the sponsoring organization. A donor can establish multiple DAFs at a single sponsoring organization.

A variety of charities sponsor DAFs, including charitable organizations formed by financial institutions for the principal purpose of offering DAFs, community foundations, universities, SOs, and other tax-exempt organizations that may have a range of endowment funds or charitable activities they support. The sponsoring organization generally distributes grants from the DAF's assets to charities engaged in direct charitable activities. The sponsoring organization might also engage in other activities to support the grant recipients or the community in other ways, i.e., maintaining DAFs may be the sole purpose of the sponsoring organization or one of many things it does. However, the DAF's assets are generally used for grant-making; the grantee organization generally provides direct charitable services.

At the time of donation, a charitable contribution deduction is generally available to the donor for contributions to an SO or a DAF. The SO or the DAF sponsoring organization owns and controls the donated assets and all investment returns from those assets. In some circumstances, a donor to an SO may be in a position to exert influence over investment and distribution of the SO's assets, e.g., if the donor serves as an officer of the SO or as a member of its governing board. As a legal matter, however, the donor has no right to control the manner in which the SO uses the particular funds contributed to the SO by the donor. In the case of a DAF, the donor is explicitly permitted to advise the sponsoring organization about how the donated funds should be invested and/or disbursed to other charities, but such advice is subject to the DAF sponsoring organization's ultimate discretion and control.

Concerns regarding donor influence or control over SOs and DAFs culminated in changes to the law included in the PPA, which also directed the Department of the Treasury (Treasury) to promulgate regulations addressing SOs.[3] Although the PPA focused largely on pension reform,

---

[2] A DAF may be contributed to by more than one donor. The donor may appoint an advisor to exercise the advisory privileges related to the DAF. When referring to advisory privileges throughout this report, the term "donor" also refers to an appointed advisor.

[3] On August 2, 2007, Treasury and the IRS issued an advance notice of proposed rulemaking, "Payout Requirements for Type III Supporting Organizations That Are Not Functionally Integrated" (72 Fed. Reg. 148) that described rules Treasury and the IRS intended to propose to implement the PPA changes to Type III SO requirements. The advance

2

it contained a substantial subtitle on charitable reform. The charitable reforms included, among others:

- **New reporting requirements for SOs.** Most SOs are now required to file IRS Form 990, "Return of Organization Exempt from Income Tax" (Form 990), a Federal return for tax exempt organizations, regardless of the amount of their gross receipts. An SO is required to list its supported organization(s); indicate whether the SO is a Type I, Type II, or Type III SO; and certify that the organization is not donor-controlled.

- **Payout requirement for non-functionally integrated Type III SOs.** Type III SOs that primarily make grants to their supported organizations—referred to as non-functionally integrated Type III SOs—will face a revised, annual payout requirement designed to ensure that a significant amount is paid to their supported organizations. Non-functionally integrated Type III SOs were newly defined in the PPA. (See the discussion below.)

- **Additional excess benefit transaction rules for SOs.** SOs are subject to new excess benefit transaction rules intended to curb loans to disqualified persons and grants, loans, compensation, and other similar payments from an SO to substantial contributors or their related parties.

- **New reporting requirements for DAFs.** Sponsoring organizations are required to report on Form 990 the total number of DAFs held, the aggregate value of assets in those DAFs, and the aggregate contributions to and grants from those DAFs during the tax year.

- **New excise taxes for DAFs.** DAF sponsoring organizations are subject to a new 20 percent excise tax on any distribution from a DAF made to an individual or to an entity either for any non-charitable purpose or if the sponsoring organization fails to exercise expenditure responsibility. In addition, any fund manager of the sponsoring organization who knowingly approves a taxable distribution is subject to a five percent excise tax on the amount of the distribution.

  There is also a new 125 percent excise tax on donors, advisors, or related parties for distributions from a DAF that benefit (more than incidentally) a donor, advisor, family member, or certain controlled entities of the donor or advisor. In addition, any fund manager that approves of such a distribution, knowing that it will confer a more-than-incidental benefit, is subject to a ten percent excise tax on the amount of the benefit.

- **Additional excess benefit transaction rules for DAFs.** DAF sponsoring organizations are subject to new excess benefit transaction rules intended to curb grants, loans, compensation, and other similar payments from a DAF to donors, advisors, or their related parties.

---

notice also solicited comments regarding the proposed rules. On September 24, 2009, Treasury and the IRS issued proposed regulations (74 Fed. Reg. 48672) addressing the requirements for Type III SOs. These proposed regulations are referred to below as the "Proposed SO Regulations." The Proposed SO Regulations state that they are proposed to be effective on the date of publication of final regulations. The text of the Proposed SO Regulations (REG–155929–06) is found on page 665 of Internal Revenue Bulletin 2009-47 at http://www.irs.gov/pub/irs-irbs/irb09-47.pdf. (Last accessed December 1, 2011.)

- **Application of excess business holdings rules for DAFs.** The PPA extended the private foundation excess business holdings rules to DAFs and also provided a definition of "disqualified person" for purposes of applying these rules to DAFs.

As part of the PPA, Congress requested that Treasury undertake a study of the organization and operation of DAFs and SOs, with specific consideration of the following:[4]

1. **Whether the Existing Deduction Rules for Contributions to DAFs and SOs are Appropriate:** Specifically, whether the deductions allowed for income, gift, or estate tax purposes for charitable contributions to DAFs and SOs are appropriate in consideration of the use of the contributed assets (including the type, extent, and timing of such use) or of the use of the assets of such organizations for the benefit of the person making the charitable contribution (or a related person).

   Donors to DAF sponsoring organizations and SOs, like donors to other public charities, are generally allowed to claim a current year charitable contribution deduction for a larger percentage of their income donated to these entities than if they had donated to private foundations.

2. **Whether DAFs Should be Subject to a Distribution Requirement:** Specifically, whether a DAF should be required to distribute for charitable purposes a specified amount (whether based on the income or assets of the fund) in order to ensure that the sponsoring organization is operating in a manner consistent with the purposes or functions constituting the basis for its exempt status.

   As discussed below, private foundations, which share some functional characteristics with DAFs, are required to distribute five percent of their assets annually.[5] Under current law, DAF sponsoring organizations have no distribution requirement for DAF assets, either at the individual DAF level or in aggregate.

3. **Whether an Advisory Role in the Investment or Distribution of Donated Funds is Consistent with a Completed Gift:** Specifically, whether the retention by a donor of rights or privileges with respect to amounts transferred to a DAF or an SO (including advisory rights or privileges with respect to the making of grants or the investment of assets) is consistent with the treatment of the transfer as a completed gift that qualifies for a deduction for income, gift, or estate tax purposes.

   Under current law, a charitable gift is not considered to be "complete"—and no charitable deduction is allowed—if the donor maintains control over the gift, its sale, or further use.

---

[4] The mandate for the study, which contains the precise language for the questions Congress posed, is found in Appendix B.

[5] Private foundations are classified as either operating or non-operating foundations. The former conduct direct charitable activities, whereas the latter tend to be grant-making entities. Non-operating foundations comprised more than 90 percent of private foundations in 2006, and grant-making non-operating private foundations comprised more than 80 percent of private foundations. In common parlance, the modifier "non-operating" is often omitted when discussing private foundations. Unless otherwise noted, the use of "private foundations" below refers to non-operating private foundations.

4. **Other Forms of Charity:** Whether the issues described in questions 1-3 are also issues with respect to other forms of charities or charitable donations.

This report presents Treasury's analysis of the questions posed by Congress. Chapter 2 contains a description of the Federal tax law treatment of charities, including SOs and DAF sponsoring organizations. Chapter 3: contains a statistical overview of SOs and DAF sponsoring organizations. Chapter 4: contains a summary of public comments that Treasury and the Internal Revenue Service (IRS) solicited and received on topics related to SOs and DAFs. In particular, Treasury and the IRS asked the public to provide input on the questions asked by Congress and to evaluate the steps taken in the PPA to improve compliance and limit abuse. Chapter 5: concludes the study with Treasury's answers to the questions posed by Congress.

Executive Summary and Major Findings

The data collected by the IRS, along with the public comments, provide the following insights:

- Charities are increasingly large and complex in terms of their operations, assets, and activities. SOs and DAFs play an important role in the charitable sector.

  - During tax year 2006, SOs received $94.1 billion in total revenue, had total expenses of $72.5 billion—including $11.5 billion in grants paid, $4.0 billion in payments to affiliates, and $46.9 billion in program expenses—and had a net worth of $226.7 billion at the end of the year. SOs that support organizations that provide medical and dental care for low-income households, work with hospital patients and employees, and conduct health research had the largest revenue, expenses, and net worth.

  - During tax year 2006, DAF sponsoring organizations received $59.5 billion in revenue, including $9.0 billion in contributions to DAFs. These sponsoring organizations had total expenses of $37.7 billion—including $5.7 billion in grants paid from DAF assets, $6.8 billion in other grants paid, and $20.7 billion in program expenses—and had a net worth of $211.3 billion at the end of the year. (Assets in DAFs are a subset of these amounts. See below.)

- Prior to tax year 2006, the data available on DAFs were very limited. Recent changes in reporting are expected to improve the data available for analysis over time.[6] Beginning with tax year 2006, the Form 990 required DAF sponsoring organizations to report the total number of DAFs they owned, the aggregate value of assets held in their DAFs, and the aggregate contributions to and grants from their DAFs. This will make it possible to calculate aggregate payout rates at the sponsoring organization level, monitor certain trends related to DAFs, and compare payout rates of Aggregate DAFs with those of private

---

[6] When new information is requested on a tax form, taxpayers often face a learning curve in filling out the form properly. As taxpayers work with their tax advisors and the IRS, the quality of the data submitted by taxpayers tends to improve over time. The analysis of Form 990 for 2006—the first year for which complete data were available for use in time for this report—indicates a similar pattern is likely to develop for information related to DAFs. See Data Appendix C for additional discussion.

foundations.[7] (Information on individual DAFs is unavailable.) Beginning with tax year 2008, sponsoring organizations report the aggregate data on their DAFs and similar accounts in a separate section.

- IRS data indicate that in tax year 2006, the 2,398 DAF sponsoring organizations had 160,000 DAFs. The assets in these DAFs were valued at $31.1 billion as of the end of tax year 2006.

  - Aggregate DAFs sponsored by the charitable arms of financial institutions (*commercial NDAFs*) had an average of $424.5 million in total assets and median assets of $58.9 million, the largest among the broad categories of organizations that sponsor DAFs.[8]

  - The average payout rate across all Aggregate DAFs in 2006 was 9.3 percent.[9] Aggregate DAFs sponsored by community foundations had an average payout rate that matched the overall average. Among the commercial NDAFs, the average payout rate was 14.2 percent. Other NDAFs had an average payout rate of 28.7 percent.

- Respondents to the solicitation for public comments noted that while it was generally true that the DAF sponsoring organizations approved most donor grant recommendations, approval was not automatic.

  - In general, sponsoring organizations reported that they have specific guidelines applicable to grants from DAFs, and they ensure that the guidelines are followed and that their donors and grantees are made aware of the restrictions applicable to them. The sponsoring organizations serve as intermediaries that match charitable needs with the charitable preferences of their donors.

- Therefore, the fact that DAFs have high approval rates for donor recommendations is not in itself indicative of donors' exerting excessive control over their donated assets. The public comments correctly point out that high approval rates for grant recommendations are not sufficient to support the claim that the gifts should not be considered "complete."

The insights above inform Treasury's answers to the questions Congress posed.

---

[7] The payout rates reported for DAFs and private foundations are not strictly comparable due to computation differences and differences in information collected on Form 990 for DAF sponsoring organizations and information collected on Form 990-PF for private foundations.

[8] DAF sponsoring organizations that have *national* reach and whose primary role is to serve as intermediaries between donors and a broad range of charities providing direct charitable services by sponsoring and maintaining DAFs and other similar charitable funds will be referred to in this study as NDAFs. The subset of NDAFs that is sponsored by charitable affiliates of financial institutions will be referred to as *commercial* NDAFs, and the NDAFs that are not sponsored by such organizations will be referred to as *other* NDAFs.

[9] The payout rate for an Aggregate DAF is calculated by dividing the total grants from DAFs at a given sponsoring organization by DAF assets available for grant-making at that sponsoring organization (i.e., the value of aggregate DAF assets at year end plus the value of grants made from DAFs during the year). The average payout rate across the Aggregate DAFs is the arithmetic mean of the payout rates across all Aggregate DAFs. For further discussion, see page 58.

- The PPA appears to have provided a legal structure to address abusive practices and accommodate innovations in the sector without creating undue additional burden or new opportunities for abuse.

- Although donors may prefer making gifts of appreciated property to SOs and DAFs, rather than to private foundations, in order to take a larger charitable contribution deduction, they may do so only if they are willing not only to part with control of the assets, but also to give the assets to organizations they do not control. Because contributions to DAF sponsoring organizations and SOs, like contributions to other public charities, are generally to organizations the donor doesn't control, the deduction rules are appropriate.

- There may be a lag between when a donor contributes assets to a DAF sponsoring organization or an SO—and may claim a charitable contribution deduction—and when the donated assets are used for direct charitable activities. The issue of the lag between contribution and final use of assets is no different at DAF sponsoring organizations and SOs than it is for other public charities that may operate charitable funds or maintain endowments. Thus, it is appropriate that the contribution deduction rules faced by donors to SOs and DAF sponsoring organizations are the same as those applicable to donors to other public charities.

- Several provisions of the Code address issues related to donor benefit. A charitable deduction is disallowed to the extent that a donor receives benefits that are of more than insubstantial value in exchange for the contribution. In addition, an organization's tax-exempt status may be revoked if it operates to benefit private interests, such as those of its donors, or if it does not further a charitable purpose. Further, the Code contains deterrents in the form of excise taxes both on a donor who receives excess benefits from a public charity and on the charity's managers if they knowingly approved the transaction conferring the benefit. The PPA also enacted new provisions in the form of taxes designed to deter SOs, DAF sponsoring organizations, and their donors from allowing donors to receive certain payments or any improper benefits from an SO or DAF.

- Compared to private foundations, the mean payout rates for Aggregate DAFs in tax year 2006 appear to be high for most categories of DAF sponsoring organizations.[10] It would be premature to recommend a distribution requirement for DAFs at this point. As more years of data become available, analysis of trends with respect to DAF sponsoring organizations and the DAF assets they administer will be possible.

- Current law disallows a charitable contribution deduction for a contribution to any charity that does not meet the standard of a completed gift, including in the case of a gift to a DAF or SO. However, as is the case with gifts to other charities, if all existing tax and other legal requirements are met, donations to a DAF or an SO may be completed gifts and become the property of the donee organization. Although donee organizations may feel an obligation to

---

[10] This is relative to the roughly five percent payout rate observed for private non-operating foundations. However, note that while these percentages provide some perspective on payout policy and practice, payout rates for DAFs and private foundations are not directly comparable because of differences in definitions of qualified expenditures, distributions, and assets reported by DAF sponsoring organizations and private foundations, which affect calculations of payout rates.

use donated funds in a manner preferred by the donor, especially when subsequent contributions may be desired, there is nothing unique about DAFs or SOs in this regard and, in fact, they have no legal obligation to follow the preference of the donor.

- As the effects of the PPA and the new regulations become clearer over time, Treasury looks forward to working with Congress to determine whether additional legislation or reporting is necessary.

Chapter 2: Description of Federal Tax Law Treatment of Charities, Supporting Organizations, and Donor Advised Funds

An organization that meets the requirements of section 501(c)(3) of the Code may be recognized as exempt from Federal income tax.[11] The requirements include that the organization must be organized and operated exclusively for religious, charitable, scientific, testing for public safety, literary, or educational purposes; to foster national or international amateur sports competition; or for the prevention of cruelty to children or animals. In addition, the organization must serve a public rather than a private interest.[12] No part of the organization's net earnings may inure to the benefit of organizational insiders,[13] and only incidental private benefits may accrue to others. Lobbying must not be a substantial part of the organization's activities, and the organization may not participate or intervene in political campaign activities.

The Code also confers a benefit on individuals and corporations who donate to section 501(c)(3) organizations in the form of a charitable contribution deduction. The rules for charitable contribution deductions are set forth in section 170 of the Code and distinguish between types of donors (individuals or corporations), types of donees (public charities or private foundations), and types of property contributed (e.g., cash, capital gain property, ordinary income property, and inventory).[14]

It is important to keep in mind that both donors—through the charitable contribution deduction—and section 501(c)(3) organizations—through the income tax exemption—receive benefits under the Code. The PPA's provisions largely affect the rules under which SOs and DAF sponsoring organizations must operate to avoid excise taxes and maintain their tax-exempt status. However, the questions Congress posed relate both to these rules and to the rules governing the tax benefits donors receive.

The legal treatment of charitable organizations in general, and SOs and DAF sponsoring organizations in particular, provides background and guidance for Treasury's answers to the Congressional questions. This chapter provides an overview of the Federal tax law treatment of the wide variety of charities—in terms of their organizational structure and charitable activity—covered by section 501(c)(3) of the Code and associated regulations. Figure 2.1 displays the classification of these charities and serves as a roadmap for the first part of the chapter. The second part of the chapter outlines the provisions of the PPA that affect SOs, DAFs, and their donors.

---

[11] To operate as a section 501(c)(3) organization, the organization generally must apply for and receive recognition of tax-exempt status by the IRS and comply with all applicable rules governing reporting and activity. Generally, houses of worship are presumed to be exempt and are not required to apply for IRS recognition of their exempt status.

[12] See Treas. Reg. § 1.501(c)(3)-1.

[13] In this context, inurement means private benefits resulting from the use of the assets of the exempt organization.

[14] Contributions made to public charities are generally subject to more favorable deduction rules than are contributions to private foundations. These rules are discussed in more detail in the following section.

Figure 2.1: Universe of Section 501(c)(3) Organizations

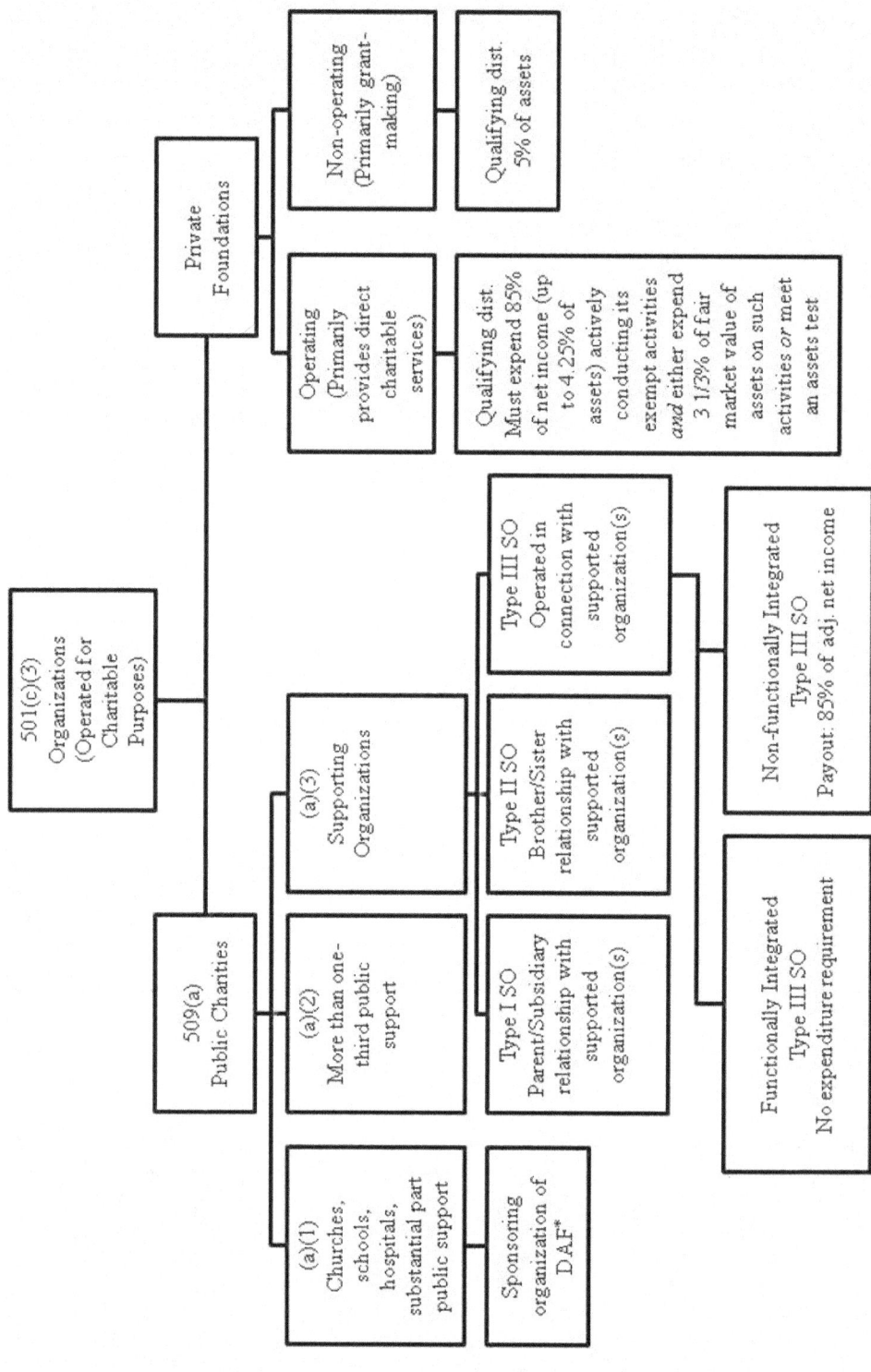

* Subject to certain restrictions, most organizations described in section 509(a) of the Code may be a DAF sponsoring organization, although most sponsoring organizations are described by section 509(a)(1) of the Code.

Public Charities vs. Private Foundations

Since 1969, a tax-exempt charity described in section 501(c)(3) is classified as either a private foundation or a public charity.[15] In general, a public charity is distinguished from a private foundation by the level of public support or oversight the organization receives. The greater the degree of public support or oversight, the greater the likelihood the organization is a public charity. Organizations that are funded and controlled by only a few donors—an individual, family, or corporation—tend to be classified as private foundations.

Section 509(a) defines the organizations that qualify for public charity status. A charitable organization that is not described in section 509(a)(1), (2), (3), or (4), outlined below, is, by default, classified as a private foundation.

- 509(a)(1): Organizations described in Code section 170(b)(1)(A) (other than in clauses (vii) and (viii)).

    - Churches, educational institutions, hospitals, medical research organizations, and organizations that normally receive a substantial part[16] of their support from direct or indirect contributions from the general public or a governmental unit.

- 509(a)(2): Organizations that normally receive more than one-third of their support from gifts, grants, contributions, membership fees, and gross receipts from the performance of activities related to their exempt function and not more than one-third of their support from investment income.

    - Museums, theaters and other organizations with support from numerous donors or government grants, or that generate revenue from their exempt function.

- 509(a)(3): Organizations that are organized and operated exclusively for the benefit of, to perform the functions of, or to carry out the purposes of one or more specified organizations described in section 509(a)(1) or 509(a)(2).

    - This defines SOs. An SO qualifies as a public charity through its relationship with the public charity (or charities) it supports. SOs are discussed further below.

- 509(a)(4): Organizations organized and operated exclusively for testing for public safety.

A charity's classification as a private foundation or a public charity has important consequences in terms of the rules under which it must operate and the tax benefits its donors receive. Private

---

[15] See the Tax Reform Act of 1969, Pub. L. 91-172 (the 1969 Act), which enacted Chapter 42 of the Code.

[16] The regulations under section 170 of the Code provide that an organization is treated as normally receiving a substantial part of its support from public sources if it meets either a one-third public support test or a facts and circumstances test. The facts and circumstances test requires that an organization receive at least ten percent of its total support from public sources and that it be organized and operated so as to attract new and additional public or governmental support on a continuous basis. The regulations set forth a number of factors that will be taken into account in the facts and circumstances analysis, including, for example, whether the organization's governing board represents the broad interests of the public or is dominated by a single donor or family. See generally Treas. Reg. § 1.170A-9T(f).

foundations[17]—typically controlled by their donors and persons related to their donors—are subject to more restrictions on their activities than public charities, including an excise tax on net investment income and mandatory distribution requirements. More specifically:

- Excise taxes are imposed on acts of "self-dealing," including sales or exchanges, or leasing of property; lending of money; and the furnishing of goods, services, or facilities between a private foundation and a disqualified person, e.g., a foundation insider. Public charities are permitted to engage in insider transactions as long as there is no *excess benefit* to the insider (i.e., the transaction is at fair market value).

- Private foundations are subject to an excise tax on their net investment income at a rate of two percent (reduced to one percent if certain requirements are met). Private foundations are also subject to excise taxes if they have excess business holdings; make jeopardizing investments; or make taxable expenditures, e.g., expenditures for lobbying or political activities and expenditures for non-charitable purposes.

- Generally, private foundations are required to pay out five percent of the fair market value of their assets (other than assets devoted to direct charitable use) as qualifying distributions to accomplish one or more of their exempt purposes.[18] Failure to meet the minimum distribution requirement triggers an excise tax.

- Private operating foundations qualify for an exemption from the mandatory distribution requirement by engaging in a certain amount of direct charitable activity. However, they remain subject to the rules related to self-dealing, excess business holdings, jeopardizing investments, and taxable expenditures and to the excise tax on investment income. Private operating foundations are generally required to expend a specified percentage of their income on their charitable activities and, if the amount expended does not exceed a minimum percentage of their total assets, to devote a certain portion of their assets to the charitable activities they conduct.[19]

- Finally, donors to private foundations face deduction limits that are generally more restrictive than those imposed on donors to public charities. Donors of certain appreciated property to public charities may take a deduction equal to the fair market value of the contributed property, while a private foundation's donor is limited to a deduction equal to the donor's basis in the property. Also donors to private foundations are subject to additional lower limits on their total charitable contribution deduction. Donors to non-operating private foundations cannot deduct more than 30 percent of their adjusted gross income (AGI) in the case of cash donations, and 20 percent of AGI in the case of donations of capital gain property. Donors to public charities and private operating foundations, however, can deduct up to 50 percent of AGI in the case of cash donations and 30 percent of AGI in the case of donations of capital gain property.

---

[17] The discussion immediately below refers both to operating and non-operating private foundations.

[18] The qualifying distribution rules are set forth in section 4942 of the Code and accompanying regulations. Certain taxes and administrative expenses can be counted toward meeting the five percent payout requirement.

[19] See generally section 4942(j)(3) of the Code and Treas. Reg. § 53.4942(b)-1.

Figure 2.2 illustrates, from a donor's perspective, the tradeoffs between establishing a public charity and establishing a private foundation. Generally, in exchange for less restrictive rules governing transactions with insiders, more generous charitable contribution deduction limits, and no distribution requirements, donors to public charities give up all control over the donated assets and generally do not control the charity. At a private foundation, donors may control the foundation and thus be able to maintain a certain amount of influence over the donated assets, but the foundation is subject to an excise tax on investment income, operational restrictions, a mandatory distribution requirement, and less generous charitable deduction rules.

Figure 2.2: Donor's Tradeoffs between Establishing or Contributing to a Public Charity versus a Private Foundation

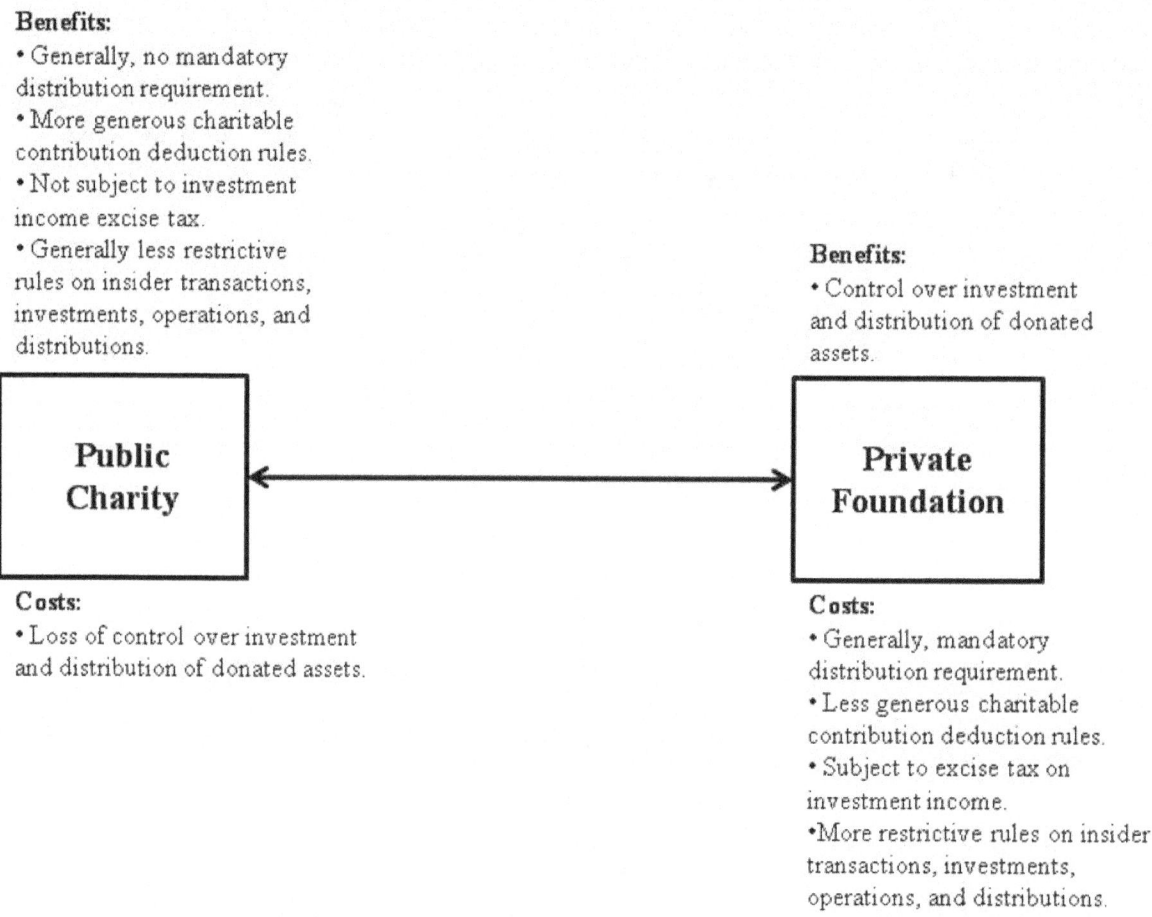

Benefits:
• Generally, no mandatory distribution requirement.
• More generous charitable contribution deduction rules.
• Not subject to investment income excise tax.
• Generally less restrictive rules on insider transactions, investments, operations, and distributions.

Public Charity

Costs:
• Loss of control over investment and distribution of donated assets.

Benefits:
• Control over investment and distribution of donated assets.

Private Foundation

Costs:
• Generally, mandatory distribution requirement.
• Less generous charitable contribution deduction rules.
• Subject to excise tax on investment income.
• More restrictive rules on insider transactions, investments, operations, and distributions.

One can think of private foundations and public charities as generally lying at either extreme of a continuum of charitable organizations. Founders of charitable organizations face the tradeoffs outlined above when determining whether to organize a public charity or a private foundation.

The tradeoffs are important to consider because public charities and private foundations can perform similar charitable activities and achieve similar philanthropic goals for their supporters. For example, although they are public charities, DAF sponsoring organizations and certain SOs may engage primarily in grant-making activities, like most private foundations, rather than providing direct charitable services. Indeed, DAFs, SOs and small private foundations all may be attractive to a donor interested in making grants to other charities. However, these alternatives allow for differing levels of donor influence or control.

Prior to enactment of the PPA, concerns were expressed that donors to some DAFs and SOs were exerting control over and personally benefitting from their donated assets.[20] To address potential influence and control by donors, the PPA strengthened the control that DAF sponsoring organizations and supported organizations can exercise over DAFs and SOs, respectively. The PPA also enacted additional operational restrictions on DAF sponsoring organizations and SOs, similar to those imposed on private foundations, including stricter rules for insider transactions and investment restrictions not generally applicable to other public charities. A summary of the major distinctions among private foundations, public charities, SOs, and DAF sponsoring organizations post-PPA is found in Table 2.1 below.

---

[20] For example, IRS Commissioner Everson's written testimony at the Senate Finance Committee's April 5, 2005 hearing, *Charities and Charitable Giving: Proposals for Reform*, included the statement: "We have found that certain promoters encourage individuals to establish purported donor-advised fund arrangements that are used for a taxpayer's personal benefit, and some of the charities that sponsor these funds may be complicit in the abuse. The promoters inappropriately claim that payments to these organizations are deductible under section 170 of the Code. Also, they often claim that the assets transferred in the funds can grow tax free and later be used to benefit the donor in the form of compensation for purported charitable projects, to reimburse them for their expenses, or to fund their children's educations." The testimony may be found at http://finance.senate.gov/imo/media/doc/metest040505.pdf. (Last accessed December 1, 2011.)

Table 2.1: Summary of Major Distinctions among Private Foundations, Public Charities, SOs, and DAF Sponsoring Organizations Post-PPA

	Charitable Contribution Deduction Limitation for Individuals[1,2]	Donor Control	Annual Distribution Requirements	Excise Taxes on Organization and/or Managers
Operating Private Foundation	Cash: 50% of AGI Capital Gain Property: 30% of AGI	Donor may control the organization.	Must expend 85% of net income (up to 4.25% of assets) actively conducting its exempt activities *and* either expend 3 1/3% of fair market value of assets on such activities *or* meet an assets test.	On acts of self-dealing with disqualified persons, investment income, excess business holdings, jeopardizing investments, taxable expenditures, and political expenditures.
Non-Operating Private Foundation	Cash: 30% of AGI Capital Gain Property: 20% of AGI	Donor may control the organization	Must expend 5% of fair market value of assets not devoted to charitable use. Grants made to non-functionally integrated Type III SOs and certain other SOs are not qualifying distributions.	On acts of self-dealing with disqualified persons, investment income, failure to meet the mandatory distribution requirement, excess business holdings, jeopardizing investments, taxable expenditures, and political expenditures.

Table 2.1: Continued

	Charitable Contribution Deduction Limitation for Individuals[1,2]	Donor Advice and Control	Distribution Requirements	Excise Taxes on Organization and/or Managers
Public Charity 509(a)(1) and 509(a)(2) (not a DAF sponsoring organization)	Cash: 50% of AGI Capital Gain Property: 30% of AGI	Donors may, but generally do not, control the organization. Donors may offer non-binding advice on investment and distribution of assets.	Medical research organizations must expend at or devote at least 3.5% of fair market value of assets for or devote more than 50% of assets to the active conduct of medical research.	On excess benefit transactions, excessive lobbying, and political expenditures.
DAF Sponsoring Organization	Cash: 50% of AGI Capital Gain Property: 30% of AGI Deduction not allowed for contributions to DAFs whose sponsoring organizations are war veterans organizations, fraternal lodges, cemetery corporations, or non-functionally integrated Type III SOs.	Donors may, but generally do not, control the organization. Sponsoring organization owns assets and returns on assets. Donor may offer non-binding investment and distribution advice.	None.	On excess benefit transactions, excessive lobbying, political expenditures, and excess business holdings in DAFs. On distributions from DAFs to individuals, or to certain organizations unless made for a charitable purpose and expenditure responsibility is exercised. On distributions from DAFs that convey a more-than-incidental benefit to a donor, advisor, family member, or controlled entity.

17

Table 2.1: Continued

	Charitable Contribution Deduction Limitation for Individuals[1,2]	Donor Advice and Control	Distribution Requirements	Excise Taxes on Organization and/or Managers
Type I SO	Cash: 50% of AGI Capital Gain Property: 30% of AGI	Donor may not control SO. SO is controlled by its supported organization.	None.	On excess benefit transactions, excessive lobbying, and political expenditures.
Type II SO	Cash: 50% of AGI Capital Gain Property: 30% of AGI	Donor may not control SO. SO is controlled by persons who control its supported organization.	None.	On excess benefit transactions, excessive lobbying, political expenditures, and excess business holdings if the SO accepts a contribution from a donor who controls a supported organization.
Functionally Integrated Type III SO	Cash: 50% of AGI Capital Gain Property: 30% of AGI	Donor may not control SO. SO is NOT controlled by its supported organization.	None.	On excess benefit transactions, excessive lobbying, and political expenditures.

18

Table 2.1: Continued

	Charitable Contribution Deduction Limitation for Individuals[1,2]	Donor Advice and Control	Distribution Requirements	Excise Taxes on Organization and/or Managers
Non-Functionally Integrated Type III SO	Cash: 50% of AGI Capital Gain Property: 30% of AGI	Donor may not control SO. SO is NOT controlled by its supported organization.	Must distribute 85% of net income to supported organizations and meet an attentiveness test. Proposed SO Regulations would revise the payout requirement to 5% of the fair market value of non-exempt use assets.[3]	On excess benefit transactions, excessive lobbying, political expenditures, and excess business holdings.

[1] Corporations may also receive a charitable contribution deduction. The rules are set forth in Section 170(b)(2) of the Code, which provides a charitable contribution limit of 10% of taxable income.

[2] In addition to the overall limitation on total charitable contribution deductions, Section 170 of the Code sets forth rules for determining the amount that may be deducted for contributions of certain types of property. These rules distinguish between types of donors (individuals or corporations), types of donees (public charities or private foundations), types of property contributed (e.g., cash, capital gain property, ordinary income property, and inventory), and in some cases, distinguish between whether or not the contributed property is used to directly further the exempt purpose of the organization.

[3] Section 1241(d) of the PPA directed the Secretary of the Treasury to promulgate new regulations under section 509 establishing a mandatory distribution requirement for non-functionally integrated Type III SOs. On September 24, 2009, Treasury and the IRS published proposed regulations. "Payout Requirements for Type III Supporting Organizations That Are Not Functionally Integrated" (74 Fed. Reg. 48672), proposing a payout requirement equal to 5% of the value of non-exempt-use assets. The regulations are proposed to be effective on the date of publication of final regulations.

SOs

An organization that is not a public charity described in section 509(a)(1) or (2) of the Code may still be classified as a public charity under section 509(a)(3) if it has a prescribed relationship with one or more public charities described in section 509(a)(1) or (2). Such an organization is an SO, and the organization(s) described in section 509(a)(1) or (2) that the SO supports is referred to as the supported organization(s).

The 1969 Act excluded SOs from classification as private foundations, and the PPA revised the statutory definition of "supporting organization." To qualify as an SO under section 509(a)(3) of the Code, an organization must satisfy three requirements:

- The organization must be organized and operated exclusively for the benefit of, to perform the functions of, or to carry out the purposes of one or more specified public charities described in section 509(a)(1) or (2).

- The organization must be: (i) operated, supervised, or controlled by; (ii) supervised or controlled in connection with; or (iii) operated in connection with one or more public charities described in section 509(a)(1) or (2).[21] This is referred to as the "relationship test."

- The organization must not be controlled directly or indirectly by one or more disqualified persons other than foundation managers and other than one or more public charities described in section 509(a)(1) or (2).

The relationship test is met if the SO maintains one of three relationships with the supported organization(s). An SO is classified as a Type I, Type II, or Type III SO based on whether its relationship with its supported organization(s) is described in subparagraph (i), (ii), or (iii) of section 509(a)(3)(B), respectively.

- A Type I SO is "operated, supervised, or controlled by" one or more supported organizations. The relationship is comparable to a "parent-subsidiary" corporate relationship in that the supported organization can direct the policies, programs, or activities of the SO. The relationship may be established by the fact that a majority of the officers, directors, or trustees of the SO is appointed or elected by the governing body, members of the governing body, officers acting in their official capacity, or the membership of one or more of the supported organizations.[22]

- A Type II SO is "supervised or controlled in connection with" one or more supported organizations. The relationship is comparable to a "brother-sister" corporate relationship in that the two organizations are under common supervision or control. The relationship may

---

[21] Section 1241(a) of the PPA amended section 509(a)(3)(B) of the Code to bring the descriptions of the three types of SO in the regulations into the Code. See Treas. Reg. § 1.509(a)-4(f)(2). Prior to the PPA, section 509(a)(3)(B) of the Code read as follows: "is operated, supervised, or controlled by or in connection with one or more organizations described in paragraph (1)or (2)."

[22] See Treas. Reg. § 1.509(a)-4(g).

be established by the fact that control or management of the SO is vested in the same persons that control or manage the supported organization(s).[23]

- A Type III SO is "operated in connection with" one or more supported organizations. The governing board of a Type III SO is not controlled by its supported organization(s) or by those who control the supported organization(s). Instead, in order to be a Type III SO, an SO must be responsive to the needs of the supported organization(s) and be significantly involved in the operations of the supported organization(s). The regulations set forth two tests—a responsiveness test and an integral part test—which must be met in order to establish that the SO meets the Type III relationship test.[24] However, because a Type III SO is not controlled by its supported organization(s), donor influence has been more of a concern in Type III supporting organizations.

DAFs

The first donor-advised fund is reported to have been created at the New York Community Trust around 1931,[25] and the popularity of this charitable-giving vehicle has grown ever since. Despite having been in use for 75 years, the term "donor advised fund" was not codified until the enactment of the PPA. A variety of charities sponsor DAFs, including charitable organizations formed by financial institutions for the principal purpose of offering DAFs, community foundations, universities, SOs, and other tax-exempt organizations that may have a range of endowment funds or other charitable activities they conduct.

In the early 1990s, a number of charities began operating DAFs as their primary or sole activity. These sponsoring organizations can be broadly classified into two types.[26] DAF sponsoring organizations that have *national* reach and whose primary role is to serve as intermediaries between donors and a broad range of charities providing direct charitable services by sponsoring and maintaining DAFs and other similar charitable funds are referred to in this study as national DAFs, or NDAFs. The subset of NDAFs that consists of the charitable affiliates of financial institutions, such as those that operate large mutual funds or retirement accounts, are referred to in this study as *commercial* NDAFs. Others with *national* reach that are not affiliated with financial institutions are referred to in this study as *other* NDAFs.

Typical features of a DAF include:

- Donors contribute to the public charity to establish or fund a DAF. The charity maintains a separate account balance for each DAF.

---

[23] See Treas. Reg. § 1.509(a)-4(h).

[24] See Treas. Reg. § 1.509(a)-4(i). The Proposed SO Regulations maintain both of these tests but propose revisions to both tests which reflect statutory changes made by the PPA and address Congressional concern that the current regulations do not ensure that there is a sufficient nexus between the SO and supported organizations.

[25] See Victoria B. Bjorklund, "The Emergence of the Donor-Advised Fund," 3 Paul Streckfus' EO Tax J. 15 (May 1998) and Victoria B. Bjorklund, "Choosing Among the Private Foundation, Supporting Organization and Donor-Advised Fund," (May 2003), p. 27, retrieved from http://www.stblaw.com/content/Publications/pub239.pdf on January 11, 2010. (Last accessed December 1, 2011.)

[26] The DAF form is flexible, and other models may develop over time.

- Contributions to the public charity sponsoring the DAF are irrevocable. The charity owns the assets held in the DAF. Contributions may qualify for an income tax deduction under section 170 at the time of the donation, governed by the deduction rules applicable to public charities. Before the PPA, the sponsoring organization's operations and assets were subject to the same rules applicable to public charities. Post-PPA, DAF sponsoring organizations are subject to additional restrictions, described below.

- The donor or an advisor designated by the donor has the right to recommend grants be made from the DAF to qualified charitable recipients. The sponsoring organization need not accept the recommendation. If it does not, it may make a reasonable effort to solicit an alternate grant recommendation.

- In contrast to a private foundation, a DAF typically affords the advantages of anonymity, which takes on two forms. First, the donee organization may receive a grant from the sponsoring organization with no reference made to the DAF from which the funds were drawn. Second, because the Form 990 does not require public charities to report distributions on a fund-by-fund basis, grants from specific DAFs are not reported separately.

- A DAF sponsoring organization typically provides the legal, administrative, and accounting work to establish and maintain several DAFs, resulting in lower start-up costs and ongoing administrative burden than with a private foundation. A sponsoring organization generally requires that all activities, including donor advice, be subject to the conditions of the charity's governing document and reserves the right to modify the DAF agreement.

- A sponsoring organization may allow the assets held in a DAF to be distributed to a charitable recipient designated by the donor upon the donor's death. A sponsoring organization also may allow a donor to appoint a successor advisor for the DAF, e.g., a spouse, child, or other descendant, who would continue to make recommendations regarding distributions from the account.

PPA Changes

The popularity of SOs and DAFs increased throughout the 1990s, and concerns regarding abuses of SOs and DAFs emerged within Congress and the Executive branch in the early 2000s.[27] The Administration's Fiscal Year 2001 budget contained a proposal to "Clarify Public Charity Status of Donor Advised Funds" and urged legislative action regarding DAFs. The Senate Finance Committee held hearings in 2004 and released a "White Paper" containing reform proposals.[28]

---

[27] For example, IRS Commissioner Everson's testimony at the Senate Finance Committee's June 22, 2004 hearing, *Charity Oversight and Reform: Keeping Bad Things from Happening to Good Charities*, referenced a purported charitable donation to an SO that was almost immediately returned to the donor in the form of an unsecured loan and "[DAF] promoters [who] encourage clients to donate funds and then use those funds to pay personal expenses, which might include school expenses for the donor's children, payments for the donor's own 'volunteer work', and loans back to the donor." See IR 2004-81, available at http://www.irs.gov/pub/irs-news/ir-04-081.pdf. (Last accessed December 1, 2011.)

[28] See Senate Finance Committee Staff, Tax Exempt Governance Proposals: Staff Discussion Draft (June 22, 2004), available at http://finance.senate.gov/imo/media/doc/062204stfdis.pdf. (Last accessed December 1, 2011.) Testimony and other information related to the Senate Finance Committee's June 22, 2004 hearing, *Charity Oversight and Reform: Keeping Bad Things from Happening to Good Charities*, can be found at

At the encouragement of the Senate Finance Committee, the Panel on the Nonprofit Sector, which was composed of 24 participants from a diverse set of non-profit organizations and assisted by several expert advisory groups, issued a report to Congress recommending legislative action by Congress and regulatory action by the IRS.[29] "Abuse of Charitable Organizations and Deductions"—with specific reference to SOs and DAFs—was listed on the IRS "Dirty Dozen" list—an annual list of notorious tax abuses—in 2005, 2006, and 2007.[30]

This line of inquiry and subsequent analysis ultimately led to a charitable reform subtitle in the PPA containing new rules and sanctions applicable to SOs and DAF donors and sponsoring organizations. The PPA enacted specific rules regarding the permissible behavior of donors, SOs, and DAF sponsoring organizations, described further below.

Changes to the Law Governing SOs

The PPA amended section 509 of the Code to codify the distinction in the regulations among the three types of SOs; defined the terms "supported organization" and "Type III supporting organization;" defined and codified the regulatory distinction between "functionally integrated" and "non-functionally integrated" Type III SOs;[31] imposed additional excess benefit transaction taxes on SOs; and subjected non-functionally integrated Type III SOs, as well as certain Type II SOs, to excise taxes on excess business holdings.

The PPA added the following new rules applicable to all SOs:

- **Automatic Excess Benefit Transactions.** The PPA expanded the definition of "excess benefit transactions" to include any grant, loan, compensation, or other similar payment from an SO to a substantial contributor, related person, or controlled entity of a substantial contributor and any loan by an SO to a disqualified person. The entire amount of the grant, loan, compensation, or other payment is treated as the excess benefit.

  - The PPA also defined the term "substantial contributor" for purposes of the new SO automatic excess benefit transaction rules as a person who contributed more than $5,000 in aggregate to the SO, if that amount is more than 2 percent of the total contributions received by the SO, and the creator of a trust.

---

http://finance.senate.gov/hearings/hearing/?id=48ca4cce-afe1-db95-0fcb-8ff9255e780a. (Last accessed December 1, 2011.)

[29] See Panel on the Nonprofit Sector, Strengthening Transparency, Governance, Accountability of Charitable Organizations: A Final Report to Congress and the Nonprofit Sector (June 2005); Panel on the Nonprofit Sector, Strengthening Transparency, Governance, Accountability of Charitable Organizations: A Supplement to the Final Report to Congress and the Nonprofit Sector (April 2006).

[30] See IR 2005-19 (Feb. 28, 2005), available at http://www.irs.gov/newsroom/article/0,,id=136337,00.html (last accessed December 1, 2011); IR 2006-25 (Feb. 7, 2006), available at http://www.irs.gov/newsroom/article/0,,id=154293,00.html (last accessed December 1, 2011); and IR 2007-37 (Feb. 20, 2007), available at http://www.irs.gov/newsroom/article/0,,id=167983,00.html (last accessed December 1, 2011).

[31] Prior to the PPA, the technical term "functionally integrated" was used as a shorthand description, but there was no statutory definition.

- **Donor Control of Supported Organizations.** A Type I or Type III SO is prohibited from accepting a gift or contribution from a person who, together with family members and 35-percent controlled entities, directly or indirectly controls a supported organization of the SO. Type II SOs that accept contributions from such donors will be subject to the private foundation excess business holdings rules.

- **Private Foundation Grants to SOs.** Grants by private foundations are not qualifying distributions if they are made to a non-functionally integrated Type III SO or to any other type of SO if a disqualified person[32] of the private foundation directly or indirectly controls the SO or a supported organization of the SO. In addition, a private foundation must exercise expenditure responsibility over any such grants.[33]

- **DAF Grants to SOs.** DAF sponsoring organizations must exercise expenditure responsibility over any distribution from a DAF to a non-functionally integrated Type III SO or to any other type of SO if a donor, advisor, or related party directly or indirectly controls a supported organization of the SO.

- **Form 990 Filing Threshold.** An SO is generally required to file a Form 990 (or Form 990-EZ) for tax periods ending after August 17, 2006, even if the SO's annual gross receipts are normally below the general Form 990 filing threshold.[34] If an SO supports a religious organization described in section 501(c)(3) of the Code and has annual gross receipts that are normally $5,000 or less, the SO is not required to file Form 990 (or Form 990-EZ). However, the SO must submit an annual electronic notice, Form 990-N ("Electronic Notice [e-Postcard] for Tax-Exempt Organizations not Required To File Form 990 or 990-EZ") for tax periods beginning after December 31, 2006. Churches, their integrated auxiliaries, and religious orders are not required to file *any* Form 990 information return or electronic notice.

- **Form 990 Reporting.** On its Form 990, an SO must list its supported organizations; indicate whether it is a Type I, II, or III SO; and certify that the SO is not controlled by disqualified persons.

- **Excess Business Holdings.** The PPA extended the excess business holdings rules to non-functionally integrated Type III SOs and to Type II SOs that accept gifts or contributions from a donor that controls a supported organization of the SO and also provided a definition of "disqualified person" for purposes of applying these rules to SOs.

The PPA imposed the following restrictions applicable only to Type III SOs:

- **Definition of Functionally Integrated.** A functionally integrated Type III SO is an SO that is not required by Treasury Regulations to make payments to its supported organization(s) due to the activities of the SO related to performing the functions of, or carrying out the purposes of, its supported organization(s).[35] Under current regulations, a functionally

---

[32] The definition of a disqualified person for private foundations is found in section 4946(a)(1) of the Code.

[33] See section 4945(d)(4) of the Code.

[34] This threshold is $50,000 for tax years beginning in 2010.

[35] See section 4943(f)(5)(B) of the Code.

integrated Type III SO is one that engages in activities that perform the functions of or carry out the purposes of its supported organization(s) and that, but for the SO's involvement, would normally be engaged in by the supported organization(s) itself.[36]

- **Strengthened Responsiveness Test.** Type III SOs must provide each of their supported organizations with such information as the Secretary may require by regulation.[37] The PPA also effectively removed the alternate means of meeting the Type III responsiveness test previously available to charitable trusts. The Proposed SO Regulations provide one responsiveness test for all Type III supporting organizations, requiring them to demonstrate that their managers have a close relationship with the leaders of their supported organization(s) and that the supported organization(s) will have a significant voice in the operations of the SO.

- **Foreign Supported Organizations.** Type III SOs may not be operated in connection with a supported organization that is not organized in the United States.

- **Payout Requirement.** Non-functionally integrated Type III SOs will be subject to a revised annual payout requirement in order to ensure that a significant amount is paid to supported organizations, to be provided in regulations.[38]

Changes to the Law Governing DAF Sponsoring Organizations

The PPA contained the following provisions regarding DAFs and their sponsoring organizations:

- **Definition of Donor Advised Fund.** A DAF is a fund or account, owned and controlled by a sponsoring organization, that is separately identified by reference to contributions of a donor or donors who retain advisory rights over the account. To qualify as a DAF, a donor or his designee must have or reasonably must expect to have advisory privileges regarding the distribution or investment of the assets held in the DAF by reason of the donor's status as a donor.[39]

- **Definition of Sponsoring Organization.** Generally, any organization described in section 170(c) of the Code—except for governmental entities and private foundations—may sponsor a DAF.[40] It must maintain at least one DAF to be classified as a sponsoring organization.

---

[36] See Treas. Reg. § 1.509(a)-4(i)(3)(ii). The Proposed SO Regulations would change the definition of functionally integrated.

[37] The Proposed SO Regulations provide that each year Type III SOs must provide to each supported organization (i) a notice identifying the type and amount of support provided by the SO, (ii) a copy of the SO's most recently filed Form 990, and (iii) a copy of the SO's governing documents, including any amendments, if not previously provided to the supported organization.

[38] Section 1241(d) of the PPA directed the Secretary of the Treasury to promulgate new regulations under section 509 establishing a mandatory distribution requirement for non-functionally integrated Type III SOs. The Proposed SO Regulations include a proposed payout requirement equal to five percent of the value of non-exempt-use assets.

[39] The definition of "donor advised fund" is provided in section 4966(d)(2) of the Code.

[40] The definition of "sponsoring organization" is provided in section 4966(d)(1) of the Code. Note that organizations that would be described in section 170(c) of the Code, but for the fact that they are organized outside the United States, may be sponsoring organizations.

- **Excise Taxes on Taxable Distributions.** The PPA imposed a 20 percent tax on the amount of a taxable distribution from a DAF.[41] The tax is imposed on the sponsoring organization. In addition, any fund manager of the sponsoring organization who knowingly approves a taxable distribution is subject to a five percent excise tax on the amount of the distribution.[42]

- **Excise Taxes on More-Than-Incidental Benefit.** The PPA imposed an excise tax on the advice of any person to make a distribution from a DAF that results in a more-than-incidental benefit to a donor, advisor, family member, or 35 percent controlled entity. The excise tax is equal to 125 percent of the benefit.[43] The tax is levied on the advisor or the recipient of the benefits resulting from the distribution. In addition, any fund manager that approves of such a distribution, knowing that it will confer a more-than-incidental benefit, is subject to a ten percent excise tax on the amount of the benefit.[44]

- **Automatic Excess Benefit Transactions.** The PPA expanded the definition of "excess benefit transactions" to include any grant, loan, compensation, or other similar payment from a DAF to a donor, advisor, family member, or 35 percent controlled entity of the donor or advisor. The entire amount of the transaction is treated as the excess benefit.

  - The PPA also defined the term "disqualified person" for transactions involving a DAF to include a donor, advisor, family member, or 35 percent controlled entity of the donor or advisor. For transactions involving a sponsoring organization, the term "disqualified person" also includes an investment advisor, family member, or 35 percent controlled entity of the investment advisor.

- **Excess Business Holdings Rules.** The PPA extended the private foundation excess business holdings rules to DAFs and also provided a definition of "disqualified person" for purposes of applying these rules to DAFs.

- **Form 990 Reporting.** Sponsoring organizations are required to report on Form 990 the total number of DAFs held, the aggregate value of assets held in DAFs, and the aggregate contributions to and grants from DAFs during the taxable year.

- **Form 1023 Disclosure.** A sponsoring organization applying for recognition of exemption must disclose to the IRS on Form 1023 ("Application for Recognition of Exemption Under Section 501(c)(3) of the Internal Revenue Code") that it maintains or intends to maintain DAFs and the manner in which the organization plans to operate them.

- **Limits on Charitable Contribution Deduction.** A charitable contribution deduction for income, gift, or estate tax purposes is allowed only for contributions to DAFs whose sponsoring organizations are not war veterans organizations, fraternal lodges, cemetery corporations, or non-functionally integrated Type III SOs. The donor must also obtain a

---

[41] A taxable distribution is any distribution to a natural person or to an entity either for any non-charitable purpose or if the sponsoring organization fails to exercise expenditure responsibility. See section 4966(a) of the Code.

[42] The maximum amount of the tax is $10,000 for any one taxable distribution.

[43] This tax will not be imposed with respect to a distribution if an "excess benefit transaction" tax has been imposed with respect to the same distribution under section 4958 of the Code.

[44] The maximum tax imposed on managers for any one taxable distribution is $10,000.

contemporaneous written acknowledgement from the sponsoring organization that the sponsoring organization has exclusive legal control over the assets contributed to the DAF.

Regulatory Guidance

In December 2006, Treasury and the IRS issued Notice 2006-109, which provides interim guidance on certain requirements enacted by the PPA that affect SOs, DAF sponsoring organizations, and private foundations that make grants to SOs.[45] In particular, Notice 2006-109 provides guidance regarding how grantors may identify whether an SO is a Type I, Type II, functionally integrated Type III SO, or non-functionally integrated Type III SO; guidance regarding whether an SO or any of its supported organizations is controlled by disqualified persons; and rules regarding the excise tax on excess benefit transactions involving SOs. It also excludes certain employer-sponsored disaster relief funds from the definition of a DAF and provides rules regarding excise taxes on payments made pursuant to educational grants awarded prior to the enactment of the PPA.

In August 2007, Treasury and the IRS issued an Advance Notice of Proposed Rulemaking (ANPRM) (Announcement 2007-87), regarding payout requirements for Type III SOs that are not functionally integrated.[46] The ANPRM described the rules Treasury and the IRS intended to propose regarding Type III SOs, including a definition of "functionally integrated Type III SO" and an annual payout requirement for non-functionally integrated Type III SOs equal to five percent of the aggregate fair market value of non-charitable-use assets.

In September 2009, Treasury and the IRS issued the Proposed SO Regulations.[47] The Proposed SO Regulations substantially revise the definition of "functionally integrated Type III SO" set forth in the ANPRM, but provide the same payout requirement for non-functionally integrated Type III SOs of five percent of the aggregate fair market value of non-charitable-use assets. Numerous comments from the public were received in response to the ANPRM and the Proposed SO Regulations. Once final regulations are issued, organizations that do not meet the revised regulatory tests or payout requirement specified in the final regulations will be reclassified as private foundations.

---

[45] The text of this Notice is found in Appendix D: .

[46] The text of Notice 2007-87 is found on page 753 of Internal Revenue Bulletin 2007-40 at http://www.irs.gov/pub/irs-irbs/irb07-40.pdf. (Last accessed December 1, 2011.)

[47] The text of the Proposed SO Regulations (REG–155929–06) is found on page 665 of Internal Revenue Bulletin 2009-47 at http://www.irs.gov/pub/irs-irbs/irb09-47.pdf. (Last accessed December 1, 2011.)

Chapter 3: Empirical Description and Analysis of SOs and DAFs

This chapter presents a statistical overview of the charitable sector. The first section provides an historical perspective on public charities and private foundations using IRS Statistics of Income (SOI) data from 1985 through 2006. The second section focuses on SOs, and the third section focuses on DAFs and their sponsoring organizations. The primary source of information for the latter sections is the SOI sample of Form 990 returns for tax year 2006, which is supplemented with information on DAF contributions and charitable deductions from individual income tax returns.[48]

Tax year 2006 was the first year that several important reporting requirements concerning DAFs and SOs were added to Form 990. SOs were required to list each of their supported organizations and the amount of support they provided to each supported organization. In addition, the form distinguished between functionally integrated and non-functionally integrated Type III SOs (hereafter "other Type III SOs").[49] DAF sponsoring organizations were asked to report the number of DAFs and the end-of-year aggregate value of their DAFs.

Public Charities and Private Foundations

Table 3.1 provides summary statistics for public charities and private foundations that filed Form 990 for selected years from 1985 through 2006.[50] Over this period, the number of returns filed by public charities nearly tripled from about 106,000 to 301,000, a compound annual growth rate of 5.1 percent per year and many times faster than the growth in the number of households.[51] Adjusted for inflation, net assets increased fourfold from $398 billion to $1.6 trillion (measured in 2006 constant dollars), while total revenue and expenses increased threefold (measured in 2006 constant dollars).

The number of private foundations increased from 31,171 in 1985 to 81,850 in 2006, a compound annual growth rate of 4.7 percent per year. During this period, the fair market value of assets of private foundations increased more than 4 times from $159.3 billion to $645.8 billion

---

[48] The SOI tax year 2006 data include returns for calendar year 2006 and returns for fiscal years ending after June 30, 2006, and before July 1, 2007. This was the most recent year for which a full tax year SOI sample of Form 990 data was available in time for use in this report.

[49] The filer is asked on line 13 on Schedule A of the 2006 Form 990 to check the box that describes the type of supporting organization. The response categories are "Type I," "Type II," "Type III-Functionally Integrated" and "Type III-Other." For purposes of clarity in the tables and ensuing discussions in this chapter, non-functionally integrated Type III SOs will be referred to as "other Type III SOs."

[50] The data include all organizations that filed Form 990. In 2006, charities that normally received gross receipts of $25,000 or less were not required to file Form 990 and are not included unless they filed voluntarily. In addition, churches and integrated auxiliaries of churches are exempted from filing, although some still do.

[51] The Form 990 filing threshold remained constant over the applicable period at $25,000 in gross receipts. Therefore, some or even most of this faster growth may be the result of inflation and rising real incomes. An increase in the filing threshold to $50,000 for tax years beginning in 2010 is expected to reduce the number of Form 990 filers.

(measured in 2006 dollars). Unfortunately, equivalent historical tax data are not available for DAFs and SOs.[52]

The share of private foundations that are operating foundations, i.e., those that do not have a payout requirement because they conduct direct charitable activities, remained fairly stable over the period, between eight and ten percent of the total. Thus, non-operating foundations, i.e., those that primarily make grants to other charities, constituted slightly more than 90 percent of all private foundations.

The closest analogue among private foundations to non-functionally integrated Type III SOs or DAFs are grant-making non-operating foundations. These foundations generally do not conduct direct charitable activities themselves but make grants to organizations that do. The inflation-adjusted value of assets held by grant-making non-operating foundations increased from $139 billion dollars in 1985 to $589 billion in 2006. For the period, grant-making non-operating private foundations held on average 90 percent of the fair market value of assets held by private foundations. Measured in 2006 dollars, the value of grants paid by these private foundations increased from $8.6 billion in 1985 to $34 billion in 2006.

The share of the non-operating foundations that are grant-making foundations remained fairly stable over the period at around 86 percent. Anecdotal reports suggest that some smaller private foundations are being advised to consider choosing to "reorganize" as DAFs by transferring all assets to a DAF and terminating the private foundation.[53]

Among private foundations, expenses (which include distributions to charitable beneficiaries) as a share of assets were either constant or slightly decreasing over the period.[54] Roughly 74 cents of every dollar of private foundation expenses were in the form of contributions, gifts, and grants. Nearly all of these expenses came from grant-making non-operating foundations. Adjusting for inflation, contributions and grants from these organizations increased from $8.6 billion in 1985 to $33.9 billion in 2006. As a share of the fair market value of assets at grant-making non-operating foundations, contributions paid out averaged roughly six percent over the period and varied between five percent and seven percent.

---

[52] Although Form 990 asked charities to self-identify as SOs throughout this period, the IRS does not believe the historical data were of sufficient quality to be published. As noted in the text, 2006 was the first year that DAF sponsoring organizations were required to report the number of DAFs they owned and the aggregate value of assets in their DAFs.

[53] The available evidence includes comments by executives of DAF sponsoring organizations cited in *The Chronicle of Philanthropy* and on the websites of DAF sponsoring organizations that provide links for those interested in making the transfer. See, e.g., Noelle Barton and Elizabeth Schwinn, "Growing Concerns and Assets: Donor-Advised Funds Gain in Popularity as Economy Softens," *The Chronicle of Philanthropy*, Vol. 20, May 29, 2008. Donor advised funds and fiscal sponsorship as alternatives to a private foundation are discussed by Gene Takagi and Emily Chan in "Alternatives to Forming a Charitable Nonprofit: A Start-Up May Not Be in Your Client's Best Interests," *Business Law Today*, July/August 2009, pp. 15-19.

[54] Expenses as a share of the book value of assets decreased from 10 percent in 1985 to 8.6 percent in 2006. As a share of the fair market value of assets, expenses were relatively stable at 7.4 percent over the period.

Table 3.1: Public Charity and Private Foundation Information Returns, and Exempt Organization Business Income Tax Returns, Selected Financial Data, 1985-2006

(dollar amounts are in millions of 2006 dollars)

	Year					
	1985	1990	1995	2000	2005	2006
Public Charities[1]						
Number of Returns	106,449	141,757	180,931	230,159	286,615	301,214
Total assets, book value[2]	710,243	997,253	1,447,592	1,820,060	2,314,905	2,549,728
Total liabilities[2]	312,557	460,480	648,881	628,261	857,688	932,011
Net assets[2]	397,686	536,773	798,712	1,191,799	1,457,216	1,617,717
Total revenue	450,063	622,918	840,091	1,008,969	1,293,696	1,370,880
Program service revenue[3]	281,540	438,906	561,080	674,520	880,409	920,222
Contributions and grants	93,522	122,036	161,773	231,886	285,291	303,168
Memberships etc.	6,290	7,174	7,786	7,758	8,837	8,979
Other	68,711	54,802	109,452	94,806	119,160	138,511
Total expenses	409,524	585,563	765,722	927,695	1,174,970	1,230,416
Net Income	40,540	37,355	74,369	81,274	118,726	140,464
Private Foundations						
Number of Returns	31,171	40,105	47,917	66,738	79,535	81,850
Non-operating foundations	28,599	36,880	43,966	61,501	72,800	74,364
Operating foundations	2,571	3,226	3,951	5,238	6,734	7,486
Total assets, book value[2]	119,721	175,065	247,670	477,018	497,514	569,302
Total assets, FMV[2]	159,299	215,946	307,629	549,378	563,719	645,810
Investments in securities	122,907	164,421	241,551	420,984	385,235	403,668
Total revenue	27,154	27,181	39,023	84,775	78,852	94,107
Total expenses	11,974	16,139	21,768	43,604	44,217	48,797
Contributions and grants[4]	8,672	12,242	15,521	32,107	32,894	34,932
Net revenue	15,180	11,042	17,256	41,171	34,637	45,310
Net investment income[5]	16,760	17,063	25,778	56,878	45,711	54,200

Table 3.1: *Continued*

	Year					
	1985	1990	1995	2000	2005	2006
Grant-making Non-operating Foundations						
Number of Returns	25,171	31,758	37,654	53,032	63,844	64,468
Total assets, FMV[2]	139,250	193,012	272,179	496,320	510,919	588,697
Total investment assets, FMV	133,389	185,966	263,219	480,497	492,426	567,761
Total revenues	23,631	23,371	33,651	72,803	67,465	82,567
Contributions received	7,767	7,477	9,464	29,794	24,583	32,142
Contributions paid	8,561	12,132	15,073	30,928	31,642	33,850
Net Investment Income	15,142	15,833	23,715	52,456	43,240	50,973

[1] Table cells report dollar amounts in millions of dollars adjusted for inflation to 2006 constant dollars using the GDP Implicit Price Deflator. Public charity returns include data reported by organizations described in Internal Revenue Code section 501(c)(3), excluding private foundations and most religious organizations. Organizations with receipts under $25,000 were not required to file.

[2] Balance sheet data are end-of-year amounts.

[3] Represents fees collected by organizations in support of their tax-exempt purposes and income such as tuition and fees at educational institutions, hospital patient charges, and admission and activity fees collected by museums and other nonprofit organizations or institutions.

[4] The amount of contributions, gifts, and grants shown reflects the amount actually disbursed, on a cash basis, for charitable purposes.

[5] Represents income not considered related to a private foundation's charitable purpose, e.g., interest, dividends, and capital gains. Foundations could be subject to an excise tax on such income.

Source: IRS, Statistics of Income Division, October 2009 - Historical Table 16, from irs.gov/taxstats

31

The data analyzed in the remainder of the chapter are from a large sample of Form 990s for tax year 2006 processed by the SOI Division of the IRS. It is important to note that 2006 represented the first year that some of this information was reported. As a result, the data may be subject to higher error rates than would be expected in later years, after organizations become more familiar with the new questions and reporting. The redesigned Form 990, which is required to be filed starting with tax year 2008, continues to include the new questions but in a new format, with the questions in new locations on the form. Thus, there might be an additional period of taxpayer adjustment, which could reduce the accuracy of the data in the initial years.

To illustrate some of the issues, 2006 was the first year that Form 990 required sponsoring organizations to report total donations to DAFs, total grants made from DAFs, the number of DAFs, and the aggregate value of the DAFs. The form also asked whether the organization maintained separate accounts or funds other than DAFs where donors had the right to provide advice on the distribution or investment of amounts in such accounts or funds. A separate question, which was also on the 2005 form, asked whether the organization maintained DAFs. Some returns reported maintaining a DAF but provided no other information about the DAF(s). Some of these organizations may have answered the question in error. Other returns reported contributions to or distributions from a DAF but did not answer "yes" to the question asking if DAFs were maintained or provide the number of DAFs or the amounts in the DAFs. In some cases, it appeared that the individuals preparing the returns did not notice the new distinction between contributions to (or grants from) DAFs and other contributions. The returns simply reported all contributions (or grants) on the first line of the sections dealing with revenue and expenses as on the prior year form. This will impact the statistics presented in the tables below, particularly for sponsoring organizations for which sponsoring DAFs is not a major portion of their charitable activity.

Corrections were made to adjust for such errors whenever possible. However, many such errors likely remain and are thus reflected in the tables that follow. Additional discussion of such technical aspects of the data is found in Data Appendix C.

SOs

Beginning with tax year 2005, SOs were required to self-identify on their Form 990 as Type I, Type II or Type III. In tax year 2006, Type III SOs were further required to self-identify as functionally integrated Type III SOs and other Type III SOs. As shown in Table 3.2, there were 8,215 Type I, 3,179 Type II, 3,441 functionally integrated Type III, and 5,972 other Type III SOs that reported their status in 2006. In addition, approximately 600 returns were filed that identified the organization as an SO but did not specify the type. In more than half of these cases, the SO type was reported on the 2007 Form 990 or the organization's website, and this latter information was used to categorize the organization in the analysis in this section.[55]

---

[55] This lack of reporting of the SO type was most common among smaller organizations, suggesting that it may have been due to confusion about the new category definitions or fear of choosing an incorrect status. More than half of the organizations not reporting their SO type in 2006 did report the type on their 2007 return.

Table 3.2: Supporting Organizations, by Type, 2006
(dollar amounts are in millions of 2006 dollars)

| Variable | Type of Supporting Organization | | | | |
	Type I	Type II	Functionally Integrated Type III	Other Type III	Total
Sources of Revenues					
Cash contributions	14,333	974	1,882	490	17,689
Non-cash contributions	2,269	183	309	1,881	4,643
Contributions type unspecified	66	8	38	13	130
Number of Returns	736	415	479	641	2,352
Contributions to DAFs (included above)	292	34	*	42	368
Total non-government contributions	16,669	1,165	2,229	2,384	22,461
Government grants and contracts	1,340	437	672	111	2,568
Program service revenue	30,072	6,203	8,388	1,315	46,036
Investment income	5,119	1,425	1,869	1,143	9,613
Realized capital gains	6,494	1,235	1,495	1,410	10,663
Other revenues	1,393	349	784	271	2,803
Total revenues	61,087	10,813	15,437	6,635	94,143
Support, Grants and Other Expenditures					
Amount of support	18,663	3,560	4,086	1,727	28,035
Grants paid by DAFs	208	42	2	40	292
Other grants paid	6,495	1,460	1,247	2,044	11,253
Assistance to individuals	274	1	1	3	278
Benefits to members	1,008	0	34	0	1,093
Payments to affiliates	3,900	113	20	12	4,044
Program expenses	29,780	7,067	9,020	975	46,868
Total executive compensation	791	292	475	102	1,663
Distributions to disqualified persons	23	*	*	0	24
Number of Returns	17	2	3	0	22
Other management expense	3,203	1,148	1,523	277	6,162

33

Table 3.2: *Continued*

Variable	Type of Supporting Organization				
			Functionally Integrated	Other	
	Type I	Type II	Type III	Type III	Total
Total expenses	46,161	10,229	12,592	3,463	72,545
Total revenue less total expenses	14,926	612	2,845	3,172	21,627
Assets and Liabilities					
Securities investments	63,554	27,650	29,292	19,479	141,340
Other investments	84,360	10,742	20,062	6,752	122,073
Total investments	147,913	38,392	49,354	26,232	263,413
Receivables from officers, etc.	7	2	127	2	137
Number reporting loans to officers, etc.	21	9	16	11	57
Number reporting loans to other disqualified persons	2	0	1	0	3
Other assets	66,176	15,772	20,003	5,887	107,942
Total assets	214,096	54,165	69,485	32,120	371,493
Tax exempt bonds liabilities	20,526	10,175	12,484	884	44,069
Number of Returns	183	99	96	7	385
Total liabilities	80,801	27,158	32,005	4,714	144,773
Net worth, end of year	133,295	27,007	37,480	27,406	226,720
Net worth, beginning of year	116,053	23,958	31,324	23,718	196,427
Total Number of Returns	8,215	3,179	3,441	5,972	21,095

Notes: Dollar amounts are in millions of dollars. A * denotes positive values less than $0.5 million. The table is based on a sample of returns weighted to reflect the total population of SOs. The 288 SOs for which the type could not be determined are not shown separately but are included in totals. The amount of support is reported on Schedule A of Form 990 and includes expenditures in the other expenditures categories. Some missing information was added, and corrections were made to reported amounts based on other available information. See Data Appendix C for additional information.

Source: IRS Statistics of Income Form 990 File, 2006

34

Type I SOs, which have a "parent-subsidiary" relationship with their supported organization(s), accounted for 39 percent of the total number of SOs in 2006, and their $214 billion in assets accounted for 58 percent of assets held by all SOs. Type I SOs received contributions of $16.7 billion, constituting about 27 percent of their total revenues of $61 billion. Investment income of $5.1 billion and realized capital gains of $6.5 billion together accounted for an additional 19 percent of revenues.

Cash contributions accounted for 86 percent of total contributions, non-cash contributions for nearly 14 percent, and the remaining 0.4 percent was not reported by type. The percentage of non-cash donations was well below the average level of non-cash charitable contributions made by individuals as observed in analyses of SOI data, suggesting that non-cash donations are relatively less important to the operations of Type I SOs.[56]

Type I SOs reported providing a total of $18.7 billion of support to their supported charitable organizations in 2006. The large amounts of program service revenues and expenses (excluding grants) illustrate that Type I SOs are significantly involved in the provision of services. Program service revenues of $30.1 billion accounted for 49 percent of revenues in 2006, while program service expenses of roughly the same amount accounted for 69 percent of expenses.[57]

Grant-making is an important activity for some Type I SOs. These organizations paid $6.7 billion in total grants during tax year 2006. This includes $208 million in grants paid from DAF assets under their control. Grants accounted for 15 percent of total expenses for these SOs. Balance sheet data of Type I SOs in 2006 show that 43 percent of the $148 billion in investment assets were allocated to securities, with the balance allocated to other types of investments. Other assets of $66 billion, including buildings and equipment, accounted for 31 percent of total assets, which may provide another indicator of the importance of the program activities of Type I SOs.

Type II SOs, which have a "brother-sister" relationship with their supported organization(s), were the least numerous type of SO in 2006. Type II SOs accounted for 15 percent of SOs. Their assets of $54.2 billion accounted for a proportionate share of assets held by all SOs.

There were fewer than half as many Type II SOs as there were Type I SOs. The Type II SOs had one-fifth the total revenue and one-fourth the total assets as their Type I counterparts. Their sources and uses of funds, however, appear similar to those of Type I SOs. Both trace more than half of revenues and expenses to program activities, rely primarily on cash rather than non-cash donations, and have investments that account for about two-thirds of total assets. The similarity

---

[56] For tax year 2006, reported non-cash charitable contributions deductions by individuals were 28.2 percent of total reported charitable contributions deductions. See "Table 2.1—Returns with Itemized Deductions: Sources of Income, Adjustments, Itemized Deductions by Type, Exemptions, and Tax Items, by Size of Adjusted Gross Income, Tax Year 2006" compiled by the IRS, Statistics of Income Division (July 2008). Retrieved from http://www.irs.gov/taxstats/indtaxstats/article/0,,id=96981,00.html#_grp2 on March 22, 2010. (Last accessed December 1, 2011.)

[57] For the analysis in this chapter, executive compensation allocated to program expenses has been subtracted out so that all executive compensation is included under "executive compensation."

to Type I SOs is not surprising given that Type II SOs have similarly close relationships with their supported charities.

There are some differences between Type I and Type II SOs evident in the data, however. In 2006, Type II SOs had more than 70 percent of their investment assets in securities, compared to 43 percent for Type I organizations. Payouts were primarily in the form of grants, with less than ten percent of that amount in the form of payments to affiliates. Program service revenues accounted for a somewhat higher percentage of total revenues for Type II than for Type I (57 percent versus 49 percent, respectively), while contributions accounted for only 11 percent of revenues for Type II as compared to 27 percent for Type I organizations.

Beginning in tax year 2006, Type III SOs were asked to self-identify as functionally integrated Type III SOs or as other Type III SOs. The 3,441 functionally integrated Type III SOs represented 37 percent of all Type III SOs but accounted for more than two-thirds of revenues and assets held by all Type III SOs.

The functionally integrated Type III SOs appear to be most similar to the Type II SOs. Contributions of $2.2 billion accounted for about 14 percent of the $15.4 billion in total revenues. As with Type I (and Type II) SOs, program activities are quite important, as program expenses accounted for 72 percent of total expenses and program revenues accounted for 54 percent of total revenues.

The 5,972 other Type III SOs are considerably different than any of the other types of SOs. Program activities are a much smaller aspect of their activities, accounting for only 28 percent of total expenses and 20 percent of total revenues. While Type I, Type II, and functionally integrated Type III SOs receive mainly cash donations, the other Type III SOs received non-cash donations accounting for 79 percent of their total donations. These SOs rely much more on investment income and capital gains than the other types of SOs: 38 percent of total revenue, compared to 22 percent for SOs overall. Capital gains of $1.4 billion accounted for 21 percent of revenue, and other investment income, totaling an additional $1.1 billion, accounted for another 17 percent of revenue. The other Type III SOs also differ from the rest of the SOs in that their net income (total revenues less expenses) of $3.2 billion was 48 percent of their total revenue for the year, compared to 23 percent for SOs overall.

Table 3.3 presents the same data as Table 3.2 but classifies the SOs into seven categories according to the industry or sector of the SO and its supported organizations.[58] The categories are education, health, human services, community benefit, philanthropic, religious (not elsewhere classified), and other. Education includes SOs that support organizations in higher education, elementary and secondary education, and other education-related activities such as libraries, scholarship funds, or specialized education such as professional education. Health includes SOs that support organizations that work with hospital patients and employees, provide

---

[58] The categorization of SOs was conducted by the SOI division of the IRS using all of the descriptive information provided on the Forms 990 for that tax year. The codes are based on the National Taxonomy of Exempt Entities (NTEE).

medical and dental care for low-income households, and conduct health research. The human services category includes SOs that support organizations that provide housing for the elderly and low-income households, food banks, boys and girls clubs, and similar youth organizations. The community benefits category primarily includes SOs that support community foundations but also SOs that support community economic development organizations and other regionally based organizations. The philanthropy category consists primarily of SOs that have been classified as grant-making organizations. The religious category includes SOs that support organizations with religious affiliations other than those that were included in the functional categories such as human services. The "other" category includes a wide variety of generally small SOs.

Table 3.3: Supporting Organizations, by Sector, 2006
(dollar amounts in millions of 2006 dollars)

Variable	Sector							
	Education	Health	Human Services	Community Benefit	Philan-thropic	Religious NEC[1]	Other	Total
Sources of Revenues								
Cash contributions	10,755	3,015	1,062	241	956	246	1,414	17,689
Non-cash contributions	170	141	61	46	3,559	215	451	4,643
Contributions type unspecified	41	48	21	9	8	0	3	130
Number of Returns	1,545	85	203	86	5	0	427	2,352
Contributions to DAFs (included above)	22	31	6	130	1	176	1	368
Total non-government contributions	10,966	3,203	1,144	296	4,523	461	1,868	22,461
Government grants and contracts	1,510	118	158	195	3	0	584	2,568
Program service revenue	4,333	33,544	2,489	1,250	439	98	3,884	46,036
Investment income	2,450	4,104	612	212	964	358	913	9,613
Realized capital gains	3,496	3,006	574	202	1,537	391	1,457	10,663
Other revenues	672	1,023	295	8	78	40	687	2,803
Total revenues	23,426	44,998	5,271	2,164	7,544	1,348	9,392	94,143
Support, Grants and Other Expenditures								
Amount of support	8,289	12,571	1,402	249	1,138	419	3,966	28,035
Grants paid by DAFs	8	3	1	101	0	177	0	292
Other grants paid	3,621	3,014	619	146	2,083	257	1,514	11,253
Assistance to individuals	41	7	12	0	3	0	215	278
Benefits to members	52	26	2	1	0	0	1,012	1,093
Payments to affiliates	3,670	168	81	14	2	0	108	4,044
Program expenses	6,522	31,924	2,740	1,408	301	169	3,805	46,868
Total executive compensation	138	1,174	115	42	75	17	101	1,663
Distributions to disqualified persons	0	23	0	0	0	0	0	24
Number of Returns	1	16	3	0	1	0	1	22

Table 3.3: *Continued*

				Sector				
Variable	Education	Health	Human Services	Community Benefit	Philan-thropic	Religious NEC[1]	Other	Total
Other management expense	627	4,306	398	90	175	49	517	6,162
Total expenses	14,711	41,317	4,035	1,823	2,658	675	7,325	72,545
Total revenue less total expenses	8,743	3,680	1,236	341	4,886	673	2,067	21,627
Assets and Liabilities								
Securities investments	25,126	58,553	11,043	3,635	19,208	6,247	17,528	141,340
Other investments	40,013	45,962	4,585	1,788	9,832	1,387	18,507	122,073
Total investments	65,138	104,515	15,628	5,423	29,039	7,634	36,035	263,413
Receivables from officers, etc	0	14	122	0	0	0	1	137
Number reporting loans to officers, etc.	0	23	20	0	2	4	8	57
Number reporting loans to other disqualified persons.	0	2	1	0	0	0	0	3
Other assets	23,177	52,572	7,445	13,647	3,457	1,523	6,121	107,942
Total assets	88,316	157,101	23,196	19,070	32,497	9,157	42,157	371,493
Tax exempt bonds liabilities	6,403	33,553	2,304	740	318	1	749	44,069
Number of Returns	51	217	81	14	3	1	19	385
Total liabilities	30,079	76,155	7,530	14,826	2,100	1,286	12,797	144,773
Net worth, end of year	58,237	80,945	15,666	4,244	30,396	7,871	29,361	226,720
Net worth, beginning of year	46,034	72,074	13,710	3,734	25,049	7,189	28,638	196,427
Total Number of Returns	6,573	4,446	3,678	802	2,283	1,224	2,088	21,095
Type I	1,899	2,169	1,688	365	658	350	1,086	8,215
Type II	916	737	724	214	99	55	435	3,179
Functionally Integrated Type III	1,369	938	539	110	223	58	205	3,441
Other Type III	2,205	579	647	114	1,303	762	362	5,972

39

Table 3.3: *Continued*

				Sector				
Variable	Education	Health	Human Services	Community Benefit	Philan-thropic	Religious NEC[1]	Other	Total

Notes: Dollar amounts are in millions of dollars. Table is based on a sample of returns weighted to reflect the total population of SOs. Organizations whose SO type could not be determined are not shown separately, but are included in totals. Asterisks denote non-zero values not disclosed to avoid taxpayer identification. Religious NEC (not elsewhere classified) includes SOs with religious affiliations that are not otherwise classified. For example, an SO supporting a church-affiliated hospital would be classified under Health. Some missing information was added, and corrections were made to reported amounts based on other available information. See Data Appendix C for additional information.

Source: IRS Statistics of Income Form 990 File, 2006.

40

As shown in Table 3.3, Type I, II, and III SOs are found in all of the industry categories of charitable organizations. The Type I SO organizational form, the most numerous type, is the most frequently used in health, human services, community benefit, and other categories. The other Type III SO form is most frequently used in the education, philanthropic, and religious organization categories.

In 2006, the 6,573 education SOs accounted for 31 percent of all SOs, while their assets of $88 billion represented 24 percent of all SO assets. Education SOs provided $8.3 billion to their supported organizations in 2006, which accounted for 30 percent of all support provided by SOs to supported organizations. Most of this support came in the form of non-DAF grants or payments to affiliates, roughly $3.6 billon of each. Education SOs were relatively less involved in direct program services. Program expenses of $6.5 billion by education SOs accounted for 14 percent of total program expenses by SOs in 2006.

Health SOs dominated the program expenses expenditure category with $31.9 billion (68 percent of total program expenses by SOs). Program expenditures by health SOs constituted 77 percent of their total expenditures and 44 percent of total expenditures across all SOs.

Philanthropic SOs were relatively more dependent on contributions, particularly non-cash contributions, than were other SOs. The most important sources of their $7.5 billion in revenue in 2006 were contributions of $4.5 billion (60 percent of revenue), realized capital gains of $1.5 billion (20 percent), and other investment income of $1.0 billion (13 percent). In contrast, contributions represent only 24 percent of revenues for all SOs. Non-cash contributions to philanthropic SOs in 2006 accounted for 79 percent of their total contributions. The prominence of donations of non-cash property and (likely) subsequent realization of capital gains is a likely indicator of the importance of donations of appreciated property to philanthropic SOs, and by extension, to their donors.

SOs provide many types of support to their supported organizations, including making direct payments and providing services or facilities for the supported organization. Data about selected activities of SOs, broken out by SO type, sector, size, and whether they reported a value for the amount of support provided, are shown in Table 3.4. Of the 21,095 SOs, 12,261 (58 percent) reported a dollar amount of support on Schedule A of Form 990. Forty-two percent of the SOs, however, did not report any amount of support on the appropriate line on their Form 990 or any payment to affiliated organizations.[59]

---

[59] In cases where no support amount was reported, the amount reported as payments to affiliates was assumed to reflect support. This would understate support to the extent that other activities of the SO also would be regarded as support. A significant number of organizations reported a support amount exactly equal to the amount reported as payments to affiliates.

Table 3.4: Reported Support and Related Activities of Supported Organizations, 2006

	Returns with Reported Support				Returns with No Reported Support				Total Returns
	Made Grants	Had Program Expenses	Grants, Help, or Programs	Total	Made Grants	Had Program Expenses	Grants, Help, or Programs	Total	
Type									
Type I	3,730	2,530	4,433	4,525	2,826	2,730	3,623	3,690	8,215
Type II	1,392	780	1,435	1,512	1,149	1,379	1,629	1,667	3,179
Functionally Integrated Type III	1,642	1,108	1,876	1,899	1,176	1,239	1,461	1,542	3,441
Other Type III	3,617	1,226	4,057	4,326	1,122	979	1,566	1,646	5,972
Total	10,381	5,644	11,801	12,261	6,477	6,570	8,566	8,834	21,095
Sector									
Education	2,671	2,160	3,628	3,733	1,936	2,305	2,749	2,840	6,573
Health	2,249	1,488	2,419	2,574	1,183	1,524	1,850	1,873	4,446
Human services	1,629	679	1,761	1,873	1,313	1,330	1,677	1,805	3,678
Community benefit	343	234	359	381	328	325	422	422	802
Philanthropic	1,758	268	1,764	1,791	459	63	466	492	2,283
Religious	685	242	807	828	379	147	396	396	1,224
Other	1,046	573	1,062	1,083	879	877	1,006	1,006	2,088
Total	10,381	5,644	11,801	12,261	6,477	6,570	8,566	8,834	21,095
Assets									
Under $100,000	1,359	1,759	2,158	2,318	1,359	1,999	2,158	2,238	4,557
$100,000 - $1 million	3,362	1,331	3,518	3,598	1,875	2,119	2,670	2,750	6,348
$1 - 10 million	3,950	1,527	4,276	4,465	2,360	1,691	2,709	2,796	7,261
$10 - 100 million	1,425	806	1,536	1,565	749	632	872	891	2,457
$100 - 500 million	224	166	241	243	106	101	124	126	369
$500 million and over	60	55	71	72	28	29	32	32	104
Total	10,381	5,644	11,801	12,261	6,477	6,570	8,566	8,834	21,095

Table 3.4: *Continued*

	Returns with Reported Support				Returns with No Reported Support				Total Returns
	Made Grants	Had Program Expenses	Grants, Help or Programs	Total	Made Grants	Had Program Expenses	Grants, Help or Programs	Total	
Revenues									
Under $100,000	3,061	2,212	4,058	4,323	2,225	2,590	3,449	3,553	7,875
$100,000 - $1 million	4,617	1,625	4,810	4,974	2,500	2,271	3,110	3,229	8,203
$1 - 10 million	2,175	1,347	2,338	2,365	1,398	1,346	1,612	1,657	4,022
$10 - 100 million	446	376	500	506	312	315	345	345	852
$500 million and over	82	85	94	94	43	47	49	49	143
Total	10,381	5,644	11,801	12,261	6,477	6,570	8,566	8,834	21,095

Notes: This table is based on a sample of returns weighted to reflect the total population of SOs. "Grants, Help or Programs" also includes benefits paid to or for members and specific assistance to individuals, as reported in the statement of functional expenses. See Data Appendix C for additional information on data and definitions.

Source: IRS Statistics of Income Form 990 File, 2006.

43

Of the 8,834 SOs that did not report a support amount, 73 percent made grants, which would necessarily have been made to or for the benefit of the supported organization. A nearly identical number reported having program expenses, which may reflect services performed for or on behalf of the supported organization. Not shown in the table is that just over one percent of these SOs reported providing benefits to members or assistance to individuals. Overall, 97 percent of the SOs that did not report a value for their support did report some kind of activity that might be considered support activity.

The new information required on Form 990 beginning in 2006 can be used to analyze potentially problematic activities by SOs. For example, in the pre-PPA period, Congress identified loans from an SO to officers, directors, trustees, and key employees of the SO as a potential abuse of SO status. (The PPA banned all such loans.) In 2006, only 57 of the more than 21,000 SOs reported such loans, and only 3 reported such loans to other disqualified persons.[60] The reported total of such loans to both groups was $137 million. In almost all cases, the amounts of the loans were small in the aggregate and represented a small share of the organizations' assets.

A new item on Form 990 required SOs to report the amounts of compensation paid or distributions made to disqualified persons. This reporting requirement applied only to arrangements beginning after August 17, 2006, which is less than half the year for calendar-year filers but almost the full year for most fiscal-year filers. Twenty-two SOs reported such distributions totaling $24 million in 2006. Almost all of this activity was conducted by Type I SOs in the health sector.

DAFs

Beginning in 1999, the *Chronicle of Philanthropy* (the *Chronicle*) has conducted an annual survey of DAF sponsoring organizations. (In addition to this annual survey, the *Chronicle* conducts broader surveys of the sector that include questions about DAFs.) The *Chronicle* sample is not scientific but is broadly representative of the larger organizations that sponsor DAFs.[61] Prior to 2005, the *Chronicle's* survey was the best source of data on DAFs, and it continues to present useful information on DAFs and their sponsoring organizations.

According to a *Chronicle* survey on large charities, in 2007, 7 of the 100 largest charities in terms of donations received were commercial NDAFs, with the largest commercial NDAF ranked 4th (after the United Way, the American Red Cross, and the Salvation Army).[62] Four community foundations in the survey were also in the top 100 charities by size; all sponsor DAFs

---

[60] The number and value of loans to disqualified persons was a new item in 2006 on the Form 990 balance sheet statement.

[61] For a recent description of the survey methodology, see Noelle Barton, "How the Chronicle's Annual Survey of Donor-Advised Funds Was Compiled," *The Chronicle of Philanthropy*, Vol. 20, May 29, 2009. The *Chronicle* notes that the survey responses may incorporate effects of the PPA on reporting, as well as on behavior. The *Chronicle* advises caution when comparing across DAF sponsoring organizations, and for the same sponsoring organization, across time.

[62] For a description of the *Chronicle's* survey of the 400 largest charities, see Noelle Barton & Elizabeth Schwinn, "Modest Gains in Giving: Donations to Large Charities rose 4.3% in 2006," *The Chronicle of Philanthropy*, Vol. 20, Nov. 1, 2007. This survey is conducted annually.

as part of their activities. In total, 87 of the largest 400 charities in 2007 sponsored DAFs, and 72 of the 87 participated in the *Chronicle* DAF survey.[63]

Nine commercial NDAFs responded in all years between 2001 and 2007, including most of the largest. Among these nine, the number of DAFs increased at a compound annual growth rate of nearly 11 percent between 2001 and 2007, far greater than the growth rate for the number of households. Assets held in these DAFs increased at a compound annual rate of 14 percent from nearly $4 billion in 2001 (a recession year) to nearly $9 billion in 2007 (just before the recession that began in December 2007). The data on DAFs sponsored by community foundations are also suggestive of sector-wide growth in the period. In most years, most responding community foundations reported positive growth rates for their Aggregate DAFs. However, it is difficult to draw more specific conclusions because the set of respondents changes from year to year.[64]

Beginning with tax year 2005, Form 990 included a question to determine whether the filing organization maintained "any separate account for participating donors where donors have the right to provide advice on the use or distribution of funds." The answer to this question provided information on those charitable organizations that properly reported to the IRS that they offered DAFs or similar funds during 2005. No additional information about the number of DAFs or their value was requested on Form 990 in 2005.

The first detailed questions about DAFs were added to Form 990 for tax year 2006. Form 990 filers were required to report the total number of DAFs, the aggregate value of the funds at year-end (across all DAFs and DAF-like funds the organization may sponsor), and contributions to and grants from the funds during the year.[65] In addition, several questions were added that affect DAFs, including whether the organization had excess business holdings in DAFs or made any taxable distributions. The redesign of Form 990 for tax year 2008 created a separate section for these questions. The redesigned Form 990 included a number of questions related to the DAF sponsoring organization's compliance with various requirements with respect to donors, donor-advisors, and grantees.

Summary information about DAF sponsoring organizations from the 2006 IRS SOI sample is shown in Table 3.5. A total of 2,398 section 501(c)(3) organizations reported that they maintained DAFs in 2006.[66] As of the end of 2006, these organizations reported having 160,000

---

[63] Ibid.

[64] Because of the sampling methods employed by the *Chronicle*, limiting the sample to only those community foundations that responded in each year reduced the information available for analysis.

[65] The filer is asked on line 4 on Schedule A of the tax year 2006 Form 990 if the organization maintained any donor advised funds. If a sponsoring organization answered "yes," it was asked on line 4f to "[e]nter the total number of separate funds or accounts owned at the end of the tax year (excluding donor advised funds included on line 4d) where donors have the right to provide advice on the distribution or investment of amounts in such funds or accounts." The sponsoring organization was asked on line 4g to enter the aggregate value of assets held in those accounts.

[66] Some additional organizations answered "yes" to the question of whether they maintained DAFs but provided no additional information. Because this question may have been answered in error, these organizations were not included in the analysis.

DAFs with a total value of $31.1 billion. For tax year 2006, DAF sponsoring organizations reported receiving a total of $9.0 billion in contributions to DAFs and an additional $11.6 billion in other contributions, for a total of $20.6 billion in contributions.[67,68] Cash and non-cash contributions to DAFs are not reported separately from other contributions to the sponsoring organizations. However, one can get some idea of the breakdown by looking at total cash and non-cash contributions to the DAF sponsoring organizations. DAF sponsoring organizations received cash contributions of $13.4 billion, or 65 percent of total contributions, and non-cash contributions of $6.9 billion, which accounted for nearly all of the remainder.[69]

---

[67] Some DAF sponsoring organizations combined their DAF and non-DAF contributions and reported them on one of the two lines. Other organizations reported DAF or non-DAF contributions on the wrong line. Corrections were made where such errors could be identified based on other information on the Form 990, the tax year 2007 Form 990, or the organization's website.

[68] DAF sponsoring organizations engage in a wide variety of activities. Maintaining DAFs may be the sole purpose of the sponsoring organization, such as in the case of a commercial NDAF, or one of many things it does, such as in the case of a community foundation or education institution.

[69] Contributions of an unspecified type totaled $0.3 billion. Approximately 17 percent of the DAF sponsoring organizations failed to report the cash and non-cash allocation of their total contributions. However, given that the unspecified contributions were less than two percent of total contributions, it can be surmised that the organizations that failed to distinguish between cash and non-cash contributions are predominantly small.

Table 3.5: DAF Sponsoring Organizations by Sector, 2006
(dollar amounts in millions of 2006 dollars)

| | NDAF | | Sector | | | | | |
Variable	Commercial	Other	Education	Community Foundations	Health	Religious NEC	Other	Total
Sources of Revenues								
Cash contributions	1,199	336	3,899	3,884	303	1,994	1,829	13,445
Non-cash contributions	2,527	91	829	1,477	38	1,273	696	6,931
Contributions type unspecified	0	56	110	12	2	73	12	266
Number of Returns	0	1	245	1	1	5	163	416
Contributions to DAFs (included above)	3,730	385	257	2,827	83	1,593	159	9,034
Number of Returns	23	19	139	510	148	296	282	1,417
Total non-government contributions	3,726	484	4,838	5,373	343	3,340	2,537	20,642
Government grants and contracts	0	5	4,339	119	28	271	423	5,184
Program service revenue	4	4	10,624	54	1,268	169	567	12,690
Investment income	340	39	3,051	1,184	84	303	168	5,170
Realized capital gains	252	27	12,624	1,370	69	280	243	14,866
Other revenues	1	-4	552	68	66	85	188	955
Total revenues	4,323	555	36,028	8,169	1,858	4,448	4,127	59,506
Grants and Other Expenditures								
Grants paid by DAFs	1,915	329	168	2,049	10	1,011	178	5,659
Number of Returns	23	19	71	512	130	282	144	1,182
Other grants paid	1	12	2,297	1,764	135	1,251	1,359	6,820
Assistance to individuals	0	0	2	19	2	4	165	192
Benefits to members	0	0	0	0	0	0	0	1
Program expenses	22	28	17,122	335	1,093	700	1,351	20,650
Total executive compensation	5	5	99	91	30	66	69	366
Distributions to disqualified persons	1	0	8	9	0	3	0	21
Number of Returns	2	0	4	4	0	6	0	16

47

Table 3.5: *Continued*

Sector

Variable	NDAF Commercial	Other	Education	Community Foundations	Health	Religious NEC	Other	Total
Other management expense	25	40	2,360	332	353	251	506	3,865
Total expenses	1,971	416	22,082	4,629	1,638	3,317	3,667	37,721
Total revenue less total expenses	2,351	139	13,946	3,541	220	1,131	459	21,787
Assets and Liabilities								
Securities investments	9,379	869	86,701	33,257	1,984	8,259	4,843	145,293
Other investments	613	398	59,019	7,446	596	2,364	1,639	72,075
Total investments	9,993	1,267	145,720	40,703	2,579	10,623	6,482	217,368
Receivables from officers, etc	0	0	6	1	0	4	1	12
Number of Returns	0	0	9	4	0	102	1	116
Other assets	230	197	31,608	2,698	1,168	2,533	5,040	43,474
Total assets	10,223	1,464	177,334	43,402	3,748	13,160	11,523	260,853
Total liabilities	321	156	38,361	3,955	797	3,495	2,447	49,533
Net worth	9,902	1,308	138,972	39,447	2,951	9,665	9,076	211,320
Net worth, beginning of year	7,066	1,138	116,666	34,067	2,603	8,154	8,186	177,881
DAF data								
Total value of DAFs	9,797	1,140	1,428	13,455	192	4,715	370	31,098
Number of individual DAFs	67,174	9,894	12,945	46,543	1,288	20,422	2,005	160,270
Total Numbers of Returns	23	19	568	607	206	368	607	2,398
Reported taxable distributions	0	0	2	76	0	0	0	78
Reported loans to disqualified persons	0	0	1	1	0	1	0	3

Notes: This table is based on a sample of returns for tax year 2006 weighted to reflect the total filing population of returns indicating that they maintain donor advised funds. Asterisks denote cells with a non-zero number of returns not disclosed to avoid taxpayer identification. Some missing information was added, and corrections were made to reported amounts based on other available information. See Data Appendix C for additional information.

Source: IRS Statistics of Income Form 990 File, 2006.

Overall, the DAF sponsoring organizations reported $5.6 billion in grants paid from DAFs. This represented 18.2 percent of the end-of-year value of the DAFs and 15.4 percent of the sum of the end-of-year value and grants from the DAFs during the year, which might be regarded as the total amount of funds available for distribution.[70] Note that while these percentages provide some perspective on payout policy and practice, they are not directly comparable to the 5-percent payout requirement for private foundations, which is based on different definitions of "qualified expenditures" and assets.

As reflected in the last column of Table 3.5, many DAF sponsoring organizations are also engaged in other charitable activities. For example, some of these organizations were primarily involved in the direct provision of charitable services. In aggregate, organizations that sponsored DAFs in 2006 received $12.7 billion in program revenues and had $20.7 billion in program expenses. In addition to grants made from DAFs, these organizations made $6.8 billion in other grants and provided $192 million in assistance to individuals.

The first columns of Table 3.5 divide DAF sponsoring organizations into seven categories based on the SOI National Taxonomy of Exempt Entities (NTEE) classifications, augmented by research using DAF sponsoring organizations' websites, the annual *Chronicle* survey of DAFs,[71] and other sources. The categories are NDAFs, which is comprised of *commercial* NDAFs and *other* NDAFs; education, including many colleges and universities; community foundations; health; religious (not elsewhere classified); and other.

The SOI data suggest that, using these definitions, there were 23 commercial NDAFs and 19 other NDAFs in 2006.[72] While they represented less than 2 percent of the number of DAF sponsoring organizations, they accounted for 48 percent of all DAFs, 35 percent of the asset value of DAFs, and 46 and 40 percent of the contributions to and distributions from DAFs, respectively.

The main characteristic of both NDAF groups is that the sponsorship of the DAFs and other similar accounts or funds generally appears to constitute the principal activity performed by the sponsoring organization. The organizations largely focus on receiving contributions, converting non-cash donations into a more liquid form, facilitating grant-making, and managing the investment of DAF assets, rather than the direct provision of charitable services.

---

[70] The total amount of assets available for grant-making is the sum of the value of assets in DAFs at the beginning of the year, contributions to DAFs made during the year, and investment income earned during the year. Mathematically, this is equivalent to the sum of the end-of-year value of DAFs plus grants made from DAF assets during the year.

[71] As noted above, the *Chronicle* has conducted an annual survey of DAF sponsoring organizations since 1999. While it includes many of the largest DAF sponsoring organizations, participation is voluntary and varies from year to year.

[72] Note that because the SOI data from Form 990 are a stratified sample, these 42 commercial NDAFs and other NDAFs are represented by 26 actual observations, several of which have sample weights greater than 1. The SOI sample includes 100 percent of the largest organizations, but declining percentages of smaller charities.

The nature of these NDAF sponsoring organizations appears clear from their assets. The value of the DAFs constituted 96 percent of the total assets of commercial NDAFs ($9.8 billion out of $10.2 billion) and 78 percent of the total assets of the other NDAFs ($1.1 billion out of $1.5 billion). Direct charitable activity appears to be minor. Program service expenses were only 1.1 percent of total expenses for commercial NDAFs and 6.7 percent of total expenses for other NDAFs.

The 2006 data from Form 990 suggest that virtually all of the activity of the commercial NDAF sponsoring organizations relates to the individual DAFs. All of the $3.7 billion in contributions were to DAFs. Donations to DAFs constituted 86 percent of the $4.3 billion in revenue at commercial NDAFs. Investment income and realized capital gains comprised nearly all of the remainder.

Nearly all of the $1.9 billion in charitable grants from NDAFs in 2006 came from DAFs. These grants constituted 97 percent of their $2.0 billion in total expenses and 22 percent of their $10.2 billion in total assets. Grants from DAFs at commercial NDAFs were 16.4 percent of the sum of the year-end value of assets and grants from those DAFs. Expenses for programs, executive compensation, and other management and fundraising activities accounted for nearly all of the remaining expenses at commercial NDAFs and were 0.5 percent of the year-end value of their DAFs.

About two-thirds of the value of the donations to DAFs at commercial NDAFs was non-cash, illustrating the importance of the ability of donors to commercial NDAFs to deduct the full fair market value of appreciated property. On the other hand, the fact that one-third of the value of donations was cash suggests that other factors and services offered by DAF sponsoring organizations also play a significant role. The net worth of commercial NDAFs increased $2.8 billion from $7.1 billion to $9.9 billion during 2006.

Overall, the impression of commercial NDAFs from the reported Form 990 data is of a relatively efficient system for the management of donated charitable funds in that reported program, management, and fundraising expenses are low relative to grants and assets under management. However, other management expenses, such as some investment fees, may have been previously netted against investment income or realized capital gains. Furthermore, while the overall payout rate on invested assets is high, no information is available on payout rates at the individual account level.

It should be noted that management expenses can be "too low" as well as "too high." Low management and program expenses could indicate that donors are receiving little oversight from the sponsoring organization, and high management and program expenses could indicate that the sponsoring organization is devoting significant resources to match donors with donee organizations. The provision of such assistance to donors and donee organizations may be an important public service provided by DAF sponsoring organizations as part of their charitable mission.

The other NDAFs are generally similar to the commercial NDAFs, although some participate in small amounts of direct programming in addition to sponsorship of DAFs.[73] While there are almost as many other NDAFs as commercial NDAFs (19 versus 23), they are much smaller; they have only $1.1 billion in DAFs—only 12 percent of the value of DAFs at commercial NDAFs. The other NDAFs received $385 million in contributions to DAFs and nearly $100 million in other non-government contributions. Unlike the commercial NDAFs, only 19 percent of the contributions to the other NDAFs were identified as non-cash.

In 2006, the other NDAFs paid out $329 million in charitable grants from DAFs and $12 million in other grants. Charitable grants from their DAFs constituted 29 percent of the year-end value of their DAFs and 22 percent of the sum of their year-end value and grants from DAFs during the year. This distribution rate was higher than the corresponding rate for commercial NDAFs (16.4 percent).

Program expenses accounted for 6.6 percent of total expenses at other NDAFs, compared to only 1.1 percent for the commercial NDAFs. The other NDAFs' management expenses, including executive compensation and fundraising costs, constituted 10.8 percent of total expenses and 3.6 percent of total assets. While these non-grant expenses were many times higher than those of the commercial NDAFs, it is impossible to determine from the data how much this reflects additional charitable activities or services (such as advice to donors and donee charities and direct charitable activity), as opposed to a lower level of efficiency. Differences may also result if the relationship between the commercial NDAF sponsoring organization and the affiliated commercial entity lead to accounting or reporting differences between the commercial NDAFs and other NDAFs.[74] The net worth of the other NDAFs increased $170 million during 2006 from $1.14 billion to $1.31 billion.

In 2006, one out of every four DAF sponsoring organizations was a community foundation. (As noted previously, community foundations were the original DAF sponsors more than 70 years ago.) Community foundations commonly raise funds and make grants to support numerous charitable initiatives in their communities, and they hold endowments for local charitable projects in a number of funds, often including DAFs. Twenty-nine percent of all DAFs are held at community foundations, second in the number of DAFs held only to commercial NDAFs. In 2006, community foundations held $41 billion of the $217 billion in investment assets held by DAF sponsoring organizations, second only to organizations in the education sector.

Community foundations received $2.8 billion in contributions to DAFs in 2006, which accounted for just over half of their $5.4 billion in total contributions and just over one-third of their $8.2 billion in revenue. Only 27 percent of community foundations' total contributions was non-cash. It is not possible, however, to tell from the reported data how much of the non-cash contribution

---

[73] In the case of the commercial NDAFs, investigations show that nearly all, if not all, of the activity of the sponsoring organization is administering DAFs. The other NDAFs are sometimes engaged in other forms of charitable endowment building through trusts and other types of funds.

[74] For example, the costs of some management and oversight services of commercial NDAFs could be included in the fees netted against investment income, while the other NDAFs perform those services and could include those costs under program expenses.

amount was made to DAFs. Investment income and realized capital gains constituted 31 percent of community foundation total revenue in 2006.

Community foundations paid out $2.0 billion in grants from DAFs and $1.8 billion in other grants for charitable purposes. In general, community foundations engage in relatively little direct charitable activity, as program expenses were only seven percent of total expenses in 2006. Overall, DAF and non-DAF grant-making constituted their primary activity, accounting for 82 percent of total expenses. Grants from their DAFs constituted 15 percent of the year-end value of their DAFs and 13 percent of the sum of their year-end value and grants from DAFs during the year.

In the remaining sectors—education, health, religious (not elsewhere classified), and other—sponsoring and maintaining DAFs are not the primary activities of the sponsoring organizations. These charities generally have as their main charitable purpose the conduct of some type of direct charitable activity. Thus, government grants and program service revenue constituted a larger portion of their revenue. For example, program service revenues constituted 29 percent of revenues for the education sector DAF sponsors (which includes colleges and schools that charge tuition), and 68 percent of total revenues for health organizations (including hospitals). Similarly, program service expenses accounted for 78 percent of total expenses for education DAF sponsors and 67 percent for health organizations.

Because the education category accounts for 68 percent of total assets of all DAF sponsoring organizations, Table 3.6 provides a closer look at this sector by separating higher education, other school-based funds, and other education related sponsoring organizations (primarily scholarship organizations). Overall, education-related DAF sponsors reported approximately 13,000 DAFs with a value of $1.4 billion at the end of tax year 2006. However, DAFs account for only a very small part of the total contributions, revenues, expenses, and assets of education-related organizations that sponsor DAFs. Universities and colleges dominate the sector when measured by revenue, expenses, total assets, the number of DAFs, or the value of assets in DAFs. The other education charities account for roughly 640 DAFs valued at $200 million at the end of 2006.

Table 3.6: Education Sector DAF Sponsoring Organizations, 2006
(dollar amounts in millions of 2006 dollars)

Variable	Colleges and Universities	Preschool, Primary, and Secondary	Other Education	Total
Sources of Revenues				
Cash contributions	3,690	34	175	3,899
Non-cash contributions	820	2	7	829
Contributions type unspecified	100	0	10	110
Number of Returns	6	0	240	245
Contributions to DAFs (included above)	215	4	38	257
Number of Returns	35	99	4	139
Total non-government contributions	4,610	35	193	4,838
Government grants and contracts	4,322	0	16	4,339
Program service revenue	10,427	138	59	10,624
Investment income	2,785	20	246	3,051
Realized capital gains	12,068	15	541	12,624
Other revenues	529	8	15	552
Total revenues	34,741	217	1,070	36,028
Grants and Other Expenditures				
Grants paid by DAFs	121	0	47	168
Number of Returns	37	1	33	71
Other grants paid	2,155	17	125	2,297
Assistance to individuals	0	2	0	2
Benefits to members	0	0	0	0
Program expenses	16,713	142	267	17,122
Executive compensation	85	3	11	99
Distributions to disqualified persons	8	0	0	8
Number of Returns	4	0	0	4
Other management expense	2,204	32	124	2,360

Table 3.6: *Continued*

Variable	Colleges and Universities	Preschool, Primary, and Secondary	Other Education	Total
Total expenses	21,310	198	573	22,082
Total revenue less total expenses	13,431	19	496	13,946
Assets and Liabilities				
Securities investments	80,993	502	5,205	86,701
Other investments	56,258	94	2,667	59,019
Total investments	137,252	596	7,872	145,720
Receivables from officers, etc	6	0	0	6
Number of Returns	7	2	0	9
Other assets	29,308	392	1,908	31,608
Total assets	166,565	988	9,780	177,334
Tax exempt bonds liabilities	9,207	26	10	9,243
Number of Returns	28	1	3	32
Total liabilities	36,782	117	1,463	38,361
Net worth	129,783	871	8,318	138,972
Net worth, beginning of year	108,703	802	7,161	116,666
DAF Data				
Total value of DAFs	1,204	14	209	1,428
Number of individual DAFs	12,302	193	450	12,945
Total Numbers of Returns	90	124	354	568
Reported taxable distributions	1	1	0	2
Reported loans to disqualified persons	1	0	0	1

Notes: This table is based on a sample of returns for tax year 2006 weighted to reflect the total filing population of education-related organizations indicating that they maintain DAFs. Some missing information was added, and corrections were made to reported amounts based on other available information. See the Data Appendix C for additional information on the data.

Source: IRS Statistics of Income Form 990 File, 2006.

Table 3.7 shows information regarding the current payout behavior of DAF sponsoring organizations. Understanding current payout behavior is a prerequisite for determining the desirability of a payout requirement for DAFs. This table shows, for each sector of DAF sponsors, the distributions of the Aggregate DAF assets, the number of DAFs at a sponsoring organization, total grants from Aggregate DAFs, payout rates for Aggregate DAFs, and the average assets held in a DAF at a sponsoring organization.[75] In order to be able to compute valid means and other statistics, this table includes only those DAF sponsoring organizations that reported both the aggregate value of their DAFs and the number of individual accounts. As a result, this table includes only 1,883 returns as compared to the 2,398 in Table 3.5. The table does include all of the NDAFs and most of the larger DAF sponsoring organizations, as an effort was made to find missing values for these cases.

---

[75] Information is only available at the Aggregate DAF level, i.e., at the sponsoring organization level and *not* at the individual DAF level. To construct the statistics for grant payout rates and assets per account, the following methods were used. The grant payout rate for each sponsoring organization was computed using Aggregate DAF values. Quantiles and means were constructed by sector using these payout rates. The average assets per DAF for each sponsoring organization was computed by dividing total assets in the Aggregate DAF by the number of accounts constituting the Aggregate DAF at the sponsoring organization. Quantiles and means were constructed by sector using these averages.

Table 3.7: Distribution of Aggregate DAF Values and Payout Rates of DAF Sponsoring Organizations, 2006

(dollar amounts in thousands of 2006 dollars unless otherwise noted)

| | Sector | | | | | | | |
| | NDAF | | | | | Religious | | |
Variable	Commercial	Other	Education	Community Foundations	Health	NEC	Other	Total
Aggregate Value of DAFs								
25th percentile	17,276	3,865	4	745	23	220	2	17
Median	58,928	17,206	18	2,916	45	656	15	388
75th percentile	214,922	62,533	71	14,430	533	8,003	376	2,932
Mean	424,494	58,517	3,777	22,282	939	24,608	786	16,513
Total (millions of dollars)	9,797	1,140	1,428	13,455	192	4,713	363	31,089
Number of DAFs								
25th percentile	51	55	1	8	2	2	1	1
Median	259	70	2	31	4	4	1	4
75th percentile	1,500	153	2	81	4	74	2	23
Mean	2,910	508	34	77	6	106	4	85
Total	67,174	9,894	12,944	46,543	1,166	20,383	2,005	160,109
Total Grants from DAFs								
25th percentile	3,138	1,693	0	10	0	0	0	0
Median	8,412	5,164	0	244	14	32	0	2
75th percentile	30,687	14,044	0	1,549	50	2,084	0	255
Mean	82,983	16,865	406	3,390	50	5,264	377	2,994
Total (millions of dollars)	1,915	329	154	2,047	10	1,008	174	637
Grant Payout Rate (%)								
25th percentile	11.0	9.0	0.0	1.9	0.0	0.0	0.0	0.0
Median	14.7	10.5	0.0	7.0	6.0	4.7	0.0	0.6
75th percentile	17.6	57.2	0.0	12.3	68.4	14.6	0.0	10.5
Mean	14.2	28.7	3.3	9.3	30.9	9.2	3.9	9.3

56

Table 3.7: Continued

| | Sector | | | | | | | |
| | NDAF | | | | | Religious | | |
Variable	Commercial	Other	Education	Community Foundations	Health	NEC	Other	Total
Average Assets per DAF (Dollars)								
25th percentile	115,925	70,271	3,946	66,529	5,750	58,001	2,020	7,558
Median	305,393	112,457	8,766	95,972	15,010	157,276	15,000	64,920
75th percentile	399,326	232,199	29,036	211,701	159,540	276,447	106,705	180,745
Mean	337,496	190,099	518,050	287,484	198,237	222,003	164,544	286,854
Total Number of Returns	23	19	378	604	205	192	462	1,883

Notes: This table is based on a sample of returns for tax year 2006 weighted to reflect the total filing population of returns indicating that they maintain donor advised funds. Returns where the number of DAFs or their value could not be determined were excluded. Average assets per DAF shows distribution statistics for the aggregate value of DAFs divided by the number of DAFs as reported. Some missing information was added, and corrections were made to reported amounts based on other available information. Some DAF sponsoring organizations reported the combined grants from DAFs and other funds, which accounts for some of the zero values for grant payouts and payout rates. See Data Appendix C for additional information.

Source: IRS Statistics of Income Form 990 File, 2006.

57

The commercial NDAF sponsoring organizations held, on average, $425 million in DAFs. The median amount of assets held at a commercial NDAF was $59 million. These values were the largest for any broad category of DAF sponsoring organization, even though other types of sponsoring organizations generally had substantial assets other than DAFs.

Commercial NDAFs were also much larger in terms of the number of individual DAFs held. While the median number of accounts was 259 for the commercial NDAFs, it was only 70 for other NDAFs and still smaller for the other categories of DAF sponsors. The numbers of accounts may be understated because some organizations reported only a single DAF, even though other information suggested they maintained multiple DAFs.

Sponsoring organizations in the education sector are often quite small. However, this category is dominated by a small number of universities with large endowment funds. Though the average value of Aggregate DAF assets is $3.8 million, the median is $18,000, and the value at the 75th percentile is $71,000.

The aggregate payout rate for a DAF sponsoring organization is computed by dividing the aggregate dollar value of grants made from DAFs during the year by the total amount of assets potentially available in the DAFs for grant-making during the year. As before, the total amount of assets available is the sum of the value of assets in DAFs at the beginning of the year, contributions to DAFs made during the year, and investment income earned during the year. This is mathematically equivalent to the value of assets in DAFs at the end of the year plus grants made from DAF assets during the year. Note that the payout rate for DAF sponsoring organizations computed below is not directly comparable to the payout rate computed by private foundations for purposes of meeting their distribution requirements.

The Aggregate DAF payout rate computed for a sponsoring organization is mathematically equivalent to the weighted average of the DAF-level payout rates, where each DAF's payout rate is weighted by its share of the sponsoring organization's DAF assets. Payout rates for DAFs with greater shares of the sponsoring organization's DAF assets are thus weighted more heavily. The Aggregate DAF payout rates of the sponsoring organizations are then used to compute the statistics shown in Table 3.7.

As discussed above, these data may contain some systematic measurement error related to the reporting of DAF assets and grants from DAF assets. Measurement issues are most likely to have occurred in the education category and the "other" category. In general, these are either small organizations or are larger organizations for which DAFs constitute a small portion of their charitable assets, and most of their expenditures are for programming or other types of grants. Although these organizations make up 45 percent of the sponsoring organizations in Table 3.7, the total number of DAFs held by these organizations is only 9 percent of the total. As a result, the reported payout rates for DAF sponsoring organizations in these categories are very low, and inferences about these organizations based on their computed Aggregate DAF payout rates are difficult to make.[76]

Because of the way the statistics are constructed—observations are at the sponsoring organization level—having low or zero payout rates for a large subset of the sponsoring organization population will mechanically lower the mean and median for the total sponsoring organization population. Although statistics are presented for each category of sponsoring organization, until all organizations have more experience with the redesigned Form 990, inferences are perhaps best made by examining those categories where DAFs constitute a larger share of the charitable activity of the sponsoring organizations.

Across all types of sponsoring organizations, the payout rate for DAF assets was 9.3 percent, on average although the median payout rate was 0.6 percent. Sponsoring organizations with Aggregate DAF payout rates of at least 5 percent account for 92 percent of the total reported value of DAF assets. Sponsoring organizations with Aggregate DAF payout rates below the 0.6 percent median account for less than three percent of the total reported value of DAF assets.

Payout rates for NDAF sponsoring organizations are greater than the overall average. Among the commercial NDAFs, the mean payout rate was 14.2 percent, and the median was 14.7 percent. Relatively large payout rates seemed to characterize most commercial NDAFs. Payout rates ranged from 11.0 percent at the 25th percentile to 17.6 percent at the 75th percentile. The payout rates were also large for the other NDAFs, ranging from 9.0 percent at the 25th percentile to 57.2 percent at the 75th percentile. The median payout rate for this group was 10.5 percent.

The mean payout rate for community foundations matched the overall average at 9.3 percent. The rate varied between 1.9 percent at the 25th percentile to 12.3 percent at the 75th percentile. The median payout rate for community foundations was 7.0 percent.

Individual DAF information is not collected, thus limiting the conclusions that may be drawn regarding activity levels in individual DAFs and the characteristics of the grants made from individual DAFs, even once more years of data become available. Individual DAF payout rates may vary widely, and aggregate payout rates may mask low payout rates (or even no payout) from a subset of individual DAFs.

Additionally, no information is currently required to be reported about the number of accounts that have made no or relatively small charitable distributions in the current year or over several years. Some DAF sponsoring organizations have specific policies to encourage DAF donor-advisers to make regular recommendations for charitable distributions. Some policies also have a contingency for the transfer of assets to a general charitable fund after notifications and a specific time period if insufficient grants have been made. DAF sponsoring organizations are not required to report information about such policies.

---

[76] Some sponsoring organizations may have misreported DAF payouts by combining DAF payouts with other grant payouts and not separately as instructed. While corrections were made for such missing information for the largest DAF sponsors, it was not possible to check all of these cases individually.

Information reported by DAF sponsoring organizations on their Forms 990 indicates that non-cash property contributions are a large share of their total donations. Table 3.8 shows data for 2005 on the types of property donated by individual taxpayers to commercial NDAFs, other NDAFs, and community foundations—the types of organizations that commonly sponsor DAFs. The table is based on a special IRS SOI study of non-cash property donations reported by individual taxpayers who filed Form 8283 for 2005. (This is the form required for individual filers claiming a deduction for non-cash donations of at least $500.) It is important to note that the table includes only those donations that could be identified as going to a DAF *sponsoring organization* by individuals who filed Form 8283 but includes non-DAF contributions to these sponsoring organizations.[77] For example, because community foundations have various types of funds, not all of the contributions to community foundations reported in the table were to DAFs at these community foundations. Nevertheless, the table provides the best data available at the sponsoring organization level.

---

[77] For example, some donations to commercial NDAFs are reported as a family's "charitable fund" and include only the family's name and not that of the DAF sponsoring organization. In addition, some DAF contributors may donate cash, donate less than $500 so that Form 8283 is not required to be filed, or donate more than $500 and fail to file the required Form 8283.

Table 3.8: Non-cash Property Donations to DAF Sponsoring Organizations, by Type of Property and Type of DAF Sponsoring Organization, 2005

(dollar amounts in thousands of 2005 dollars)

Type of Property	Number of donations	Amount of Donations by Type of DAF Sponsoring Organization				
		Commercial NDAF	Other NDAF	Other DAF	Community Foundation	All
Corporate stock	41,419	1,281,766	226,914	23,287	1,199,822	2,731,788
Mutual funds	4,884	164,965	8,076	165	46,207	219,413
Other securities	531	54,361	15,278	252	102,178	172,069
Real estate	218	1,724	4,841	0	103,358	109,924
Clothing and household items	142	0	0	0	129	129
Other and unknown	1,657	6,710	178	1,176	10,700	18,764
All property	48,851	1,509,526	255,287	24,880	1,462,394	3,252,087

Notes: DAF sponsoring organizations and types of property donations are identified using taxpayer descriptions on Form 8283. The "other and unknown" category includes art and collectibles, air miles, investment partnership interests, miscellaneous other items, and items for which no description was provided.

Source: IRS Statistics of Income, Form 8283 Study, 2005.

A total of about 49,000 deductions valued at $3.3 billion were identified as being made to these types of organizations. Deductions for donations of corporate stock of $2.7 billion, mutual funds of $219 million, and other securities of $172 million accounted for 96 percent of the total amount of non-cash deductions. Real estate donations account for an additional $110 million, or 3.4 percent, almost all of which reflects donations to community foundations.

DAF Account Requirements at Commercial NDAFs

This section examines the characteristics of commercial NDAFs. The information in this section is predominantly from the public websites of many of the major commercial NDAF sponsoring organizations, supplemented by comments made to the *Chronicle* as part of its annual study.

In characterizing the nature of the activities of NDAFs, factors to consider include the initial contribution required, the minimum account balance, the minimum value of additional contributions, the minimum grant amounts, and account and investment fees. DAF sponsoring organizations vary considerably in the ways they market their DAFs to potential philanthropists and clients. To open a new DAF, commercial NDAFs generally required initial contributions ranging from $5,000 to $25,000. In contrast, a small set of NDAFs has chosen to focus on the most affluent potential donors. For example, in 2007 one organization reported "aggressively pursuing donations from hedge fund managers and those who hold shares of corporate equity," while another also reported shifting some focus away from its traditional client base of small to midsized donors toward those with more assets.[78]

DAF sponsoring organizations compete for donors and donor contributions. For example, in 2006, one large sponsoring organization decreased its initial contribution requirement from $10,000 to $5,000, specifically to expand access to less affluent donors.[79] The sponsoring organization reported that, after decreasing the initial contribution threshold, more than 30 percent of the new accounts opened were funded with amounts between $5,000 and $10,000.[80]

Other institutions have taken more creative approaches to participate in this growth area. One investment bank that does not have an affiliated DAF sponsoring organization offers interested customers the opportunity to establish a DAF at one of many listed community foundations. Donated assets remain under the management of the investment bank's affiliated charitable organization but belong to the sponsoring community foundation.[81] Another sponsoring organization has established DAFs for local firms that enable employees of the participating firms to contribute to a DAF through payroll deductions. At least one sponsoring organization specializing in planned giving sponsors DAFs specifically to enable donors to contribute illiquid, but valuable, property that the donor's charity of choice would otherwise find difficult to accept.

---

[78] Noelle Barton & Peter Panepento, "A Surge in Assets: Donor-Advised Funds are Growing Exponentially," *The Chronicle of Philanthropy*, Vol. 19, May 3, 2007.

[79] Several respondents to the request for public comments argued that DAFs "democratize" philanthropy because a DAF account can be started with a much smaller amount than would be required to establish a private foundation.

[80] Noelle Barton & Peter Panepento, "A Surge in Assets: Donor-Advised Funds are Growing Exponentially," *The Chronicle of Philanthropy*, Vol. 19, May 3, 2007.

[81] See Debra Blum, "Companies Compete on Donor Funds," *The Chronicle of Philanthropy*, Vol. 14, May 30, 2002.

Long-term capital gains on donated appreciated stock and real property, including gains that are built-in at the time of donation, are not taxed, which enhances the value to donors of the charitable deduction of donated property, relative to other uses. The *Chronicle* reported that many DAFs are opened with donations of stock. For example, one sponsoring organization reported that donated stock accounted for about 70 percent of all contributions in 2005.[82] Of the 11 NDAF sponsoring organizations on the list of the largest 400 charities in 2006, 4 received at least 50 percent of their contributions in non-cash donations.[83] Five large community foundations also received more than 50 percent of their contributions in non-cash gifts in the same year.[84]

Information about minimal account balances and other characteristics was collected from the websites of eight major commercial NDAFs. This set includes the largest commercial NDAFs and most of the assets held by commercial NDAFs. Initial contribution requirements ranged from $5,000 to $25,000. Once an account was opened, two commercial NDAFs required donors to maintain minimum account balances of $2,500 and $5,000. Another commercial NDAF had no minimum balance requirement but levied an additional account maintenance fee if the balance fell below $15,000. The minimum additional contribution varied considerably across these sponsoring organizations. Two had no minimum amount for additional contributions. Others required minimum contributions ranging from $250 to $5,000, with three requiring contributions of at least $500.

All eight commercial NDAFs imposed a minimum on the size of grants their donors could recommend. The amounts ranged from $50 to $500, with $250 being the most common floor. One sponsoring organization required (of itself) that the Aggregate DAF must give away five percent of its assets each year, much like a private foundation, but it did not impose this requirement on individual DAFs. Fees on small accounts at these 8 commercial NDAFs ranged from 0.5 percent to 1 percent, though the definition of "small" varied from $100,000 to $1 million. Reported investment fees in addition to the account management fees varied from 0.25 percent to 2.75 percent.

Conclusions

This chapter has provided an overview of the revenue, expenses, and assets of DAF sponsoring organizations and SOs based on currently available information. The primary source of information was the Form 990s submitted for tax year 2006. This was the first year that IRS asked for additional detail about SOs and DAFs and was most recent year of data available in time for use in this report. As a result, the analysis is limited in scope. However, it provides the

---

[82] Leah Kerkman, Noelle Barton, & Candie Jones, "A Soaring Year," *The Chronicle of Philanthropy*, Vol. 18, May 4, 2006.

[83] Noelle Barton & Elizabeth Schwinn, "Modest Gains in Giving: Donations to Large Charities rose 4.3% in 2006," *The Chronicle of Philanthropy*, Vol. 20, Nov. 1, 2007.

[84] The Chronicle notes that this may be an undercount because of the way some charities calculate the value of gifts of stock. Noelle Barton & Elizabeth Schwinn, "Modest Gains in Giving: Donations to Large Charities rose 4.3% in 2006," *The Chronicle of Philanthropy*, Vol. 20, Nov. 1, 2007.

best snapshot of the activities, behaviors, and finances of these organizations. The redesign of Form 990 will lead to more extensive information available for analysis beginning for tax year 2008. The quality of the responses is expected to increase as filers become more familiar with the legal and reporting requirements related to the PPA. As more years of data become available, improved monitoring and analysis of trends within the charitable sector in general and with respect to SOs, DAFs, and DAF sponsoring organizations in particular will be possible.

Chapter 4: Public Comments on SOs and DAFs

In connection with this report, in Notice 2007-21, Treasury and the IRS solicited public comments on the organization and operation of SOs and DAFs. The following questions were asked:[85]

1. What are the advantages and disadvantages of donor advised funds and supporting organizations to the charitable sector, donors, sponsoring organizations, and supported organizations, compared to private foundations and other charitable giving arrangements?

2. How should the amount and availability of a charitable contribution deduction for a transfer of assets to a donor advised fund or a supporting organization, and the tax-exempt status or foundation classification of the donee, be determined if:

    a. the transferred assets are paid to, or used for the benefit of, the donor or persons related to the donor (including, for example, salaries and other compensation arrangements, loans, or any other personal benefits or rights)?

    b. the donor has investment control over the transferred assets?

    c. there is an expectation that the donor's "advice" will be followed, or will be the sole or primary consideration, in determining distributions from, or investment of the assets in, the supporting organization or the donor advised fund?

    d. the donor or the donee has option rights (e.g., puts, calls, or rights of first refusal) with respect to the transferred assets?

    e. the transferred assets are appreciated real, personal, or intangible property that is not readily convertible to cash?

3. What are the effects or the expected effects of the PPA provisions (including the § 4958 excess benefit transaction tax amendments applicable to donor advised funds and supporting organizations) on the practices and behavior of donors, donor advised funds, sponsoring organizations, supporting organizations and supported organizations?

4. What would be appropriate payout requirements, and why, for:

    a. donor advised funds?

    b. funds that are excepted from donor advised fund treatment by statute or by the authority of the Secretary, but for which the donor retains meaningful rights with respect to the investment or use of the transferred amounts?

    c. supporting organizations?

    d. any other types of charities?

5. What are the advantages and disadvantages of perpetual existence of donor advised funds or supporting organizations?

---

[85] Notice 2007-21, released on February 6, 2007, contains the questions. The text of Notice 2007-21 is found on page 611 of Internal Revenue Bulletin 2007-09 at http://www.irs.gov/pub/irs-irbs/irb07-09.pdf (last accessed December 1, 2011) and also in Appendix E .

6. What other types of charitable giving arrangements give rise to any of the above issues?

Fifty-five responses to Notice 2007-21 were received from a variety of sources: NDAFs, community foundations, SOs, professional and advocacy groups, and individuals. The breakdown of the respondents is provided in Table 4.1 below.

Table 4.1: Public Comments to Notice 2007-21, by Type of Respondent

Respondent Type	Number of Responses
National Association	10
Community Foundation	11
Private Individual	10
NDAF	5
SO	6
Private Foundation	6
Law Firm	6
Accounting Firm	1
Total	**55**

This chapter provides an overview of the comments received. Most respondents generally agreed that SOs and DAFs play a useful role in the charitable sector. However, opinions diverged on specific questions. The descriptions below merely report the responses. No effort was made to confirm or deny the accuracy of the statements or claims made by the respondents.

General Comments about SOs

Compared to the high level of respondent interest in DAFs, relatively few respondents to Notice 2007-21 addressed issues related to SOs. Many who did respond to the Notice furnished comments applicable both to DAFs and SOs. However, numerous comments were received in response to the ANPRM and the Proposed SO Regulations addressing issues related to SOs. To the extent that those comments were also responsive to Notice 2007-21, they are discussed in this report.

Respondents generally praised the relative benefits of SOs to the supported organizations compared to the benefits that charities derive from DAFs and private foundations. Unlike a private foundation or a DAF, an SO is expressly established for the support of one or more supported organizations, although the formal relationship between the SO and its supported organization can take a variety of forms. One respondent described the difference as follows: DAFs are donor-focused, while SOs are, by definition, focused on the interests of their supported organizations. Respondents pointed to the "unique connection" between the SO and its supported organizations and argued this makes the SO "closer" to its supported organizations— and thereby more committed to the supported organizations' purposes and goals—than a private foundation would be. Another respondent noted that the representation of the supported organization on the SO's board of directors brings a sense of immediacy to the needs of the supported organization and that this encourages distributions.

In addition, public charities use SOs for a variety of reasons, including liability protection, the provision of specialized expertise, management flexibility, and economies of scale over a discrete aspect of the charity's (or the charitable system's) operations. Some respondents said some SOs operate as endowment funds that work with the supported organizations to fund recurring or special needs that may not be amenable to normal fundraising.[86] Another respondent described how, in the case of Type III SOs, the independent management of the SO allows the SO to choose effectively among competing priorities at the supported charity, which the charity may not have the objectivity to do on its own.

General Comments about DAFs

There is a consensus among the respondents that DAFs have been a helpful development for donors in the charitable sector. They point to the recent growth in the number of DAFs and value of the assets held in those DAFs as evidence that DAFs facilitate meeting donors' philanthropic objectives. Many respondents argued that the appealing features of DAFs have led to an increase in total charitable giving, though they provided no data in support of this claim.

DAFs provide some benefits relative to private foundations because the latter can be costly to establish and maintain. Several NDAFs and community foundations stressed the role that economies of scale play in keeping the administrative costs of DAFs low relative to private foundations; the sponsoring organizations are able to spread large fixed costs across a large number of DAFs. An NDAF cited, for example, simplified and centralized recordkeeping and reporting.

Along these lines, an umbrella organization that supports grant-makers in various aspects of foundation management argued that DAFs offer efficiencies that cannot be matched by private foundations and that professional investment managers or consultants may be too costly for private foundations to utilize. This sentiment was echoed by another respondent, who said DAFs are accessible to donors who could not otherwise afford the kind of philanthropic advice the sponsoring organizations provide. This has "democratized philanthropy," according to several NDAFs, community foundations, and advocacy groups; DAFs have expanded the opportunity to participate in philanthropy—private initiatives for public good—to segments of society farther down the wealth distribution.[87]

These economies of scale also improve tax administration, according to an NDAF. In contrast to private foundations, all reporting for DAFs is the responsibility of the sponsoring organizations, which under current law are not required to report details about the operations of individual DAFs. Some respondents argued the consolidated reporting means there are fewer organizations for the IRS to monitor and fewer forms to process.

Other respondents viewed the consolidated reporting less favorably. One claimed that under current law, DAFs are "virtually invisible to tax authorities and nonprofit regulators" and expressed concern that the PPA had done nothing to alleviate this "problem." Another

---

[86] Asbestos removal from one charity's facilities was cited as an illustration of this function.

[87] The initial minimum balance for DAFs varies between $5,000 and $25,000 at commercial NDAFs.

respondent described DAFs as "a world of hidden philanthropy that merits significantly updated disclosure" and stressed that "without individual level reporting, there will be no adequate way for the IRS to determine" if a charitable purpose is being pursued and if the DAFs' managers are complying with the law. As evidence, the respondent stated the IRS does not even know how many accounts there are.[88] A recent report by the Government Accountability Office (GAO) reiterated this perspective and recommended more detailed data collection.[89]

Donor Advice and Control

Comments from community foundations stressed how their staffs work with donors to match philanthropic desires with community needs. They argued that their staffs of professional grant-makers have intimate knowledge of community needs, knowledge that is unavailable to most small foundations and NDAFs. One community foundation argued that the movement of assets toward NDAFs might be a movement away from "foundations that are truly focused on philanthropy within their narrow regions of interest." Another stated that the NDAF's purpose is "to continue to control assets" and pointed to an inherent tension between the incentives of NDAF financial advisors and charitable purposes.

A set of donors praised the research and vetting expertise of their sponsoring organization's staff. In contrast, one charity complained that charities often have difficulty gaining access to community foundation resources because DAF donors, who are often not disclosed publicly, are insulated from community needs by community foundation managers. Further, it is argued that small charities are even more insulated from donors who use commercial NDAFs because of the perceived lack of commitment of the NDAF to any local community.

The degree of donor involvement in grant-making was a prominent topic in the public comments. Both NDAF and community foundation respondents uniformly praised the advisory role donors have in the grant-making process. They argued this increases donor interest and engagement, which they further claim motivates donors to increase their charitable giving. A consortium of community foundations said that the more a donor is engaged, the more thoughtful is the grant-making. A president of a private foundation declared that donor advice is "what makes [DAFs] work."

A group of donors to a community foundation wrote that the advisory role DAFs afford them facilitates family philanthropy and the involvement of the donors' children in grant-making suggestions. Others suggested that a fund in a family's name or a fund in memoriam for a family member could be sufficient stimulus to encourage donations by other family members.

---

[88] The new reporting requirements mandated by the PPA require sponsoring organizations to report on Form 990 the total number of DAFs owned at the end of the tax year, the aggregate value of assets held in DAFs at the end of the tax year, and the aggregate contributions to and grants made from DAFs during the tax year. See section 6033(k) of the Code.

[89] "Tax-Exempt Organizations: Collecting More Data on Donor-Advised Funds and Supporting Organizations Could Help Address Compliance Challenges," GAO, GAO-06-799, July 2006. The 2006 Form 990 incorporates some of the changes recommended in the GAO report.

The expectation that a donor's advice will be followed was an issue of particular interest to respondents writing about DAFs. Sponsoring organizations noted that while it is generally true that they approve most donor recommendations, approval is not automatic. In general, sponsoring organizations mentioned that they have specific guidelines applicable to grants from DAFs, and they ensure those guidelines are followed. For example, an NDAF stated that every grant recommendation is reviewed to ensure the proposed recipient is a section 501(c)(3) organization and that the grant is a qualified grant. It also noted that its grant recommendation form and its letter to grant recipients make it clear that it does not allow grants that fulfill pre-existing pledges or personal obligations, pay for political or lobbying activities, or confer tangible benefits to the donor-advisor. A community foundation wrote that its donors sign agreements stating that the donors have non-binding rights to recommend grants and that the community foundation can reject any suggestion it believes is inappropriate for any reason. As a result, they feel the donor has no expectation the advice will be blindly followed in all circumstances.

No respondent reported ongoing disagreements with donors over the appropriateness of potential grants, and all respondents said that, in general, donor advice was followed. However, one respondent was critical of the relationship between the donor and the sponsoring organization of the DAF. The respondent expressed concern that many such arrangements "appear to give DAF donors de facto control over investment and distribution decisions."

Donor retention of investment control over donated assets was a point of concern among NDAF respondents. Some noted that if a donor retains actual control over investment of the donated assets, the gift may not be complete and, therefore, a denial of a charitable deduction would be appropriate. Most agreed that a donor should not have investment control but suggested it should be permissible for a donor to make recommendations concerning how assets should be invested, provided the sponsoring organization retained actual control. Others noted that many donors have experience in investment management and that it should be appropriate to allow that expertise to be used.

Some NDAF sponsoring organizations stated that they allow donors to recommend investment advisors under certain conditions. For example, one NDAF sponsoring organization allows donors of more than $250,000 to recommend an investment advisor who, if utilized, determines the investment allocation (including investments in individual stocks). The allocation, however, must be in compliance with the sponsoring organization's investment guidelines. This compliance requirement was mentioned by other NDAFs as well. In general, the respondents supported the ability of a donor to choose from a limited number of investment options offered by the sponsoring organization.

Charitable Contribution Deduction

Issues related to donor control surfaced throughout comments related to charitable contribution deductions. The views of the respondents varied on whether it is appropriate to allow a deduction when the donor retains significant rights with respect to the donated property, such as a call right or a right of first refusal upon resale. Many DAF sponsoring organizations said they do not accept property subject to such conditions, and several called into question whether the gift could be considered complete if such rights encumbered the property.

Other respondents saw the difficulty with gifts subject to such rights as merely one of determining the appropriate value of the property and, therefore, the amount of the deduction that may be claimed. They reasoned that an option changes the value of the asset the donor is giving up and thus should affect the amount of the deduction. If a donor has a call right that, if exercised, obligates the charity to resell the asset to the donor, the value of the gift is reduced. The general view of this group of respondents is that the deduction, even at a lower value, should remain available, provided that the charity retains control of the property that is subject to the conditions. Conversely, if a charity has a put right that, if exercised, obligates the donor to repurchase the asset from the charity, the value of the gift should be increased, according to one respondent.

Most respondents were opposed to changing the deduction rules for contributions of real, personal, or intangible property that is not readily convertible to cash. Some did not see this as a problematic area if the current appraisal standards are enforced. Others argued that any further restrictions should be applied to all charities, not exclusively to DAF sponsoring organizations and SOs. A prevalent theme throughout the comments was that much of the country's wealth is in non-cash property. It is the only type of asset that is available to some donors who wish to donate substantial amounts to charity, and it is more important to have the value of these assets ultimately available for charity than to be concerned with the possible delay of liquidation.

Many charities that provided comments stated that they do not accept illiquid property, while others accept such assets only when they are confident they can liquidate the property quickly. Some charities have guidelines governing when to accept or reject gifts of illiquid property, with consideration given to value, likelihood of appreciation, marketability, carrying costs, liability issues, whether the property produces income, and whether there are unrelated business income tax consequences from holding the property. Charities that accept illiquid property often attempt to liquidate the assets as quickly as possible, but many delay a sale in order to obtain a higher price. One charity argued that, in some cases, maintaining the illiquid asset as part of the charity's endowment may be the most beneficial option for the charity. Some community foundations stressed their expertise in liquidating property on behalf of their donors.

Finally, a number of respondents addressed issues related to assets being paid to or used for the benefit of donors or related parties. Most NDAF respondents claimed that their rules do not permit the use of assets by or for the benefit of the donor. Further, they believe that the new rules in sections 4958 and 4967 of the Code added by the PPA address potential abuses in this area and that no further statutory changes are needed.

With respect to both DAFs and SOs, a minority of respondents favored loss of or a reduction in the donor's contribution deduction if the assets are used by the donor subsequent to the making of the gift. One respondent questioned whether a loan back to a donor by either a DAF sponsoring organization or an SO should be treated as an incomplete gift that would cause the loss of a deduction for the loaned amount; if so, the respondent argued that the IRS has sufficient authority under current law to deny the deduction. Another respondent stated that there should be no conditions on gifts and that any use by the donor may suggest that no contribution has actually been made.

Distribution Requirements

Currently, private non-operating foundations are subject to a minimum payout requirement of five percent of the value of their non-charitable use assets; administrative expenses count toward the payout requirement. Unless certain asset tests are met, private operating foundations generally must spend between 3 1/3 percent and 4.25 percent of the value of their non-charitable use assets annually on the active conduct of their charitable programs and medical research organizations generally must expend 3.5 percent of the value of their endowments on the active conduct of medical research. Certain Type III SOs are required to expend 85 percent of their net income annually to benefit or support their supported organizations. Notice 2007-21 requested comments on the merits of imposing an annual payout requirement on DAFs and SOs, revising the payout requirement for certain SOs, and potentially expanding the annual payout requirement to other SOs. Most respondents confined their remarks to DAFs and SOs, although some responses were expressly broadened to include private foundations and funds that are not, by definition, DAFs. In general, the respondents did not suggest a different treatment for those entities than for DAFs and SOs.

Some respondents that favored extending the payout requirement imposed on private non-operating foundations to DAFs and SOs argued that the similarity of purpose among the three types of funds and organizations merited similar treatment. In general, supporters of a payout requirement were concerned that funds could build up in DAFs and SOs in perpetuity, without actually resulting in charitable works. They argued that DAFs make it easy for donors to accumulate assets without the restrictions and oversight the law places on private foundations. With respect to SOs, some respondents claimed that some SOs are unwilling to act without express instructions from the donors, thus limiting disbursements.

A few respondents questioned whether the documented increase in the assets held by DAFs and SOs meant a decrease in the funds that are spent on actual charitable programs, though evidence was not provided. Additional reporting requirements on Form 990—disclosure of the total amounts of contributions to and grants from DAFs—should help in evaluating this claim. To this end, one sponsoring organization recommended that no payout requirement should be considered until several years of these data are available for analysis.

Among the proponents of a payout requirement, there was a range of opinion about how the requirement should be specified. Suggested payout rates were in the two to ten percent range. Opinions varied on whether administrative expenses should be included or excluded when determining this rate. There was further divergence when it came to accommodating the use of a DAF to save for a large grant.

Some respondents opposed to payout requirements appealed to individual rights. They argued that donors and the entities they support should choose the appropriate payout level. Further, they maintained that no payout should be required of any type of charitable entity or fund, including private foundations.

Opposition to payout requirements also came from those arguing that endowments play an important function in promoting the charitable efforts of community foundations and supported charities. These respondents stressed that DAFs and SOs are important tools for building and maintaining endowments. They described how endowments are a source of grants for large projects like endowed chairs, capital investments, and other projects requiring multi-year commitments. They argued that endowments provide stability and consistency in funding that helps these types of charities and projects succeed and that annual payout requirements would make endowment-building and maintenance more difficult.

Along the same vein, some respondents claimed that by separating the donation to the DAF from the ultimate grant-making, DAFs benefit charities by "smoothing" their charitable distributions over the business cycle and by offsetting the tendency of donors to give less when economic conditions are unfavorable. As evidence, the respondents stressed that, even though contributions to DAFs decreased during a recent economic down-turn, distributions to charities from the DAFs did not decrease.[90] Advocates of DAFs argued that operating charities benefit from the existence of DAFs because this giving and grant behavior of donor-advisors ensures that grant funds are available when they are most needed.[91]

Payout Requirement for All SOs

Some respondents favored imposing a payout requirement similar to that of private foundations on all SOs or on all charitable organizations. Some advocating a payout requirement for all SOs recommended payout rates lower than five percent, including rates as low as two percent. Others recommended that the payout rate for all SOs be set above the five percent private foundation payout rate and that administrative expenses not be permitted to count toward the SO payout requirement. (One such respondent recommended abolishing Type III SOs altogether.) Several respondents favored extending the five percent payout requirement applicable to private foundations to all charitable entities, while an additional respondent recommended that a ten percent payout rate be applied to all charities in order to force them to do more to accomplish their exempt purposes and to prevent non-operating charities from having a perpetual existence.

Respondents who opposed extending an annual payout requirement to all SOs offered a variety of reasons. Some stated that the governing bodies of the SOs, not the government, are in the best position to assess spending. Others claimed that a payout requirement on all SOs would inhibit the flexibility of SOs. SOs serve a wide range of beneficial purposes, they argued, many of which are not suited to a payout requirement. Still others maintained that a payout requirement would discourage non-cash gifts or force rapid "fire sales" of non-cash assets at severely reduced prices. Finally, respondents suggested that imposing an annual payout requirement could jeopardize the continued existence of SOs and could actually reduce the amount of distributions available for charitable purposes over time. These arguments can be summarized by saying that,

---

[90] Once several years of data are available from the redesigned Form 990, analysis of how contributions to and grants from DAFs move with the business cycle can be conducted to evaluate these claims.

[91] Few operating charities responded to the Notice's request for comments, and none that furnished comments discussed this pattern of behavior.

in an effort to meet the payout requirement, SOs would be forced to make decisions and take actions that may not be in the best interest of their supported organization(s).

Payout Requirement for Non-functionally Integrated Type III SOs

Many respondents favoring a specific payout rate for SOs confined their discussion to non-functionally integrated Type III SOs. The comments summarized in this subsection apply specifically to such organizations.

Critics noted that, under the current income-based payout requirement, it is possible for donors to hold funds indefinitely in an SO and thereby avoid ever using the funds for a charitable purpose. Some respondents favored a five percent payout rate based on the value of non-charitable use assets, while allowing administrative expenses to be included in the calculation. This is equivalent to the requirement for private non-operating foundations. One respondent argued for exceptions for unique circumstances, such as a buildup of funds to support a specific project, or sufficient time to dispose of illiquid assets to avoid fire sales. Another respondent urged that the rate not exceed five percent, as this would encourage excessive risk-taking in the SO's investment portfolio.

Several respondents expressed doubt that a five percent payout rate was low enough to assure asset growth and existence of the SO in perpetuity; they recommended lower payout rates.[92] In addition to jeopardizing the SO's existence, some of these respondents noted that imposing a five percent payout rate could actually result in a lower distribution of assets for charitable purposes over time. Of the respondents who expressed concern about a five percent payout rate, some proposed alternative payout rates (most commonly, the alternatives proposed were between three and one-third and four percent, noting that such a payout rate would be consistent with the payout rates imposed on other types of charitable organizations, such as private operating foundations and medical research organizations). Some cited the need to factor in an inflation rate of up to three percent on top of investment earnings. Another respondent suggested a requirement similar to that of a private operating foundation. Several respondents suggested that the payout rate be based on a multi-year moving average of asset values in order to reduce the effects of market volatility.

Three particular recommendations reflected the hope shared by many respondents that the current rates of spending would not be seriously altered by new rules or regulations. For example, one organization that currently pays out 100 percent of its income responded that it does not want to see a payout rate that exceeds this rate of giving. Another organization argued against a payout rate exceeding two percent because that would lead to a fire sale liquidation of its large non-cash assets.

Payout Requirement for DAFs

Most of the comments applying specifically to DAFs were submitted by community foundations and NDAFs, and nearly all discussed why an annual payout requirement was unnecessary. They stressed that current Aggregate DAF payout rates well exceed the historic rate of grant-making

---

[92] One respondent in this group suggested the payout rate could be applied to all types of SOs, not just Type III SOs.

by private foundations. According to these respondents, annual distribution rates are near 20 percent for NDAFs and are somewhat less for community foundations. Annual distribution rates for private foundations hover above the five percent minimum requirement.

One NDAF reported that many of its donor-advisors choose distribution rates that will lead to a decrease in assets over time. The NDAFs described the restrictions they have in place to ensure that the behavior of their donor-advisors is consistent with charitable intent. For example, one reported reserving the right to transfer DAF assets to a general fund if too many grant requests are denied, and most reported having procedures to "force" grants when none has been made over a certain period of time. They also wrote that virtually all of their donor-advisors behave well and that they rarely need to take actions to ensure their policies are met. Consequently, most responding DAF sponsoring organizations and all NDAFs were against imposing a payout requirement, even though a subset of individual DAFs may distribute less than the five percent of assets required of a private foundation.

Most respondents, even those opposed to a mandatory payout requirement, felt that a five percent payout rate could be accepted if it were applied to the aggregate DAF holdings of the sponsoring organization and not to the individual DAFs. The NDAFs argued that monitoring of the individual accounts would be inefficient and expensive, which would ultimately decrease the funds available for grants. A number of respondents argued that a mandatory payout could be counter-productive and even reduce overall giving. This would occur if donors and advisors viewed the minimum required level as the appropriate giving norm. As evidence, they pointed to the clustering of foundation distribution rates near five percent and argued that this occurs because private foundations view the minimum as both a floor and a ceiling.

Some respondents did favor the imposition of payout rates on individual DAFs. In general, they felt that similar treatment to private foundations was appropriate because donors use DAFs and private foundations for similar purposes. These respondents were concerned about the accumulation of assets for undefined charitable purposes and thought required payouts could mitigate such accumulations. These comments applied to DAFs, SOs, and private foundations.

Distribution Requirements and Perpetual Existence

The arguments over whether DAFs, SOs, and private non-operating foundations should have a payout requirement also touch on issues related to family legacies and the perpetual existence of such funds and arrangements. In general, those favoring perpetual existence of DAFs and SOs support requirements of less than five percent or no payout requirements and believe that the opportunity to create and manage endowments is one of the strengths of DAFs and SOs (as well as private foundations). Many respondents argued that perpetual existence of DAFs allows donors to create a permanent income stream for their favorite charities. Further, because the DAFs can exist indefinitely, successive generations can support emerging needs within the community without the expense of creating a new giving vehicle in each generation. With respect to SOs, most respondents stressed the importance of a permanent and reliable funding source for charities that an endowment provides. They argued that because the supported charities exist perpetually, the need to support them will also exist for an indefinite period.

One foundation questioned the argument that building endowments now was necessary to protect future giving. The respondent argued that in a market economy, new wealth would always be created to take the place of charities and foundations that dissolve. Consequently, greater distributions for direct charitable support now will not necessarily be detrimental to the sector in the long term. This foundation suggested creating incentives for accelerated payouts. Another respondent asked, "If the need is now, why wait?"

In contrast, some respondents viewed the buildup of endowments and perpetual existence as detrimental to charitable purposes. One claimed that perpetual existence for DAFs, SOs, and other arrangements was "a mistake" because it leads to an emphasis on "accretion rather than distribution of assets." Others argued that organizations eventually lose sight of their original goals and become more focused on internal finances than on mission.

Those who favor limiting the lifespan of these funds or arrangements argued mandatory payouts were a way to limit endowment-building and, hence, the lifespan of charities and donor control. This group of respondents worried about drift from the original charitable mission of the fund or arrangement over time and the neglect of current community needs. Others argued that the decision on how long a fund or arrangement should exist is best determined by the particular arrangement or individual involved; these respondents pointed to the individual rights of donors and their successors.

Many community foundations described policies and structures that limit the advisory role of their donor-advisors and their descendents to two generations. Thereafter, the assets become part of a general fund.

Expected Effects of the PPA

The PPA enacted changes to the rules governing DAFs and SOs. In general, the new rules were aimed at improving accountability and curtailing abuse. For example, certain types of transactions that had been permitted are now prohibited.

Notice 2007-21 solicited comments on the effects that the new rules would have on practices and behaviors in the charitable sector. The most common criticism was a lack of clarity in the new rules that the respondents hoped would be resolved by regulations. Clear rules are necessary so that DAF sponsoring organizations and SOs can stay compliant with the law with minimal additional burden. One respondent stated that the PPA left a "cloud of suspicion" hanging over DAFs and SOs and warned that the PPA could have long-term effects on charitable giving.

Effects on SOs

Some respondents welcomed the changes in the PPA because of the oversight the new rules will bring to the sector, particularly for non-functionally integrated Type III SOs. A number of respondents differentiated these entities in their comments from other types of SOs. One respondent, who thought that non-functionally integrated Type III SOs should be abolished, wrote that because the relationship between the supported organization and the SO is the "flimsiest," the "likelihood of abuse [is] the greatest." A private foundation also pointed to abuse prior to the passage of the PPA and thought that with adequate enforcement of the new rules, abusive practices would diminish.

Like DAF sponsoring organizations, some SOs expressed frustration with the new sanction on compensation to donors and related persons and the inability of SOs to reimburse donor expenses. One respondent stated that many employment relationships had been terminated as a result of the changes brought about by the PPA.

Some comments referred to the uncertainty caused by the lack of a definition of a functionally integrated Type III SO in the PPA and expressed the need for guidance.[93] Several respondents identified particular concerns that they believe should be addressed in the guidance defining functionally integrated Type III SOs.

Finally, as with DAFs, some respondents stressed that the PPA has reduced the attractiveness of SO status, particularly Type III SO status. According to several respondents, some SOs are converting or are considering converting to private foundation status. Further, they argue, some new organizations are structuring themselves as private foundations instead of SOs.

Effects on DAFs

A small number of respondents wrote positively about the changes in the PPA. They believe that the changes will bring much needed clarity to DAF management and improve the ability of the IRS to monitor the funds. They also encouraged further clarification through regulation.

Many community foundations and advocacy groups stated the new PPA rules would create significant administrative costs. They warned that the additional resources used to ensure compliance would have a "chilling effect" on grant-making and create confusion concerning DAFs that would discourage their use. In contrast, the NDAFs reported that the PPA changes were likely to have minimal effects on their operations because their policies and procedures already prevent most of the newly prohibited transactions.

A set of DAF sponsoring organizations stressed that there would be increased administrative costs incurred from determining which organizations are non-functionally integrated Type III SOs and from determining which individuals control the supported organizations of Type I and II SOs.[94] One respondent went so far as to say that one SO was researching whether staff indemnification is appropriate in light of exposure to the excise taxes under new section 4966 of the Code.

Some respondents objected to the PPA changes because they had been using the assets in their DAFs in ways that are no longer permitted post PPA enactment, e.g., using DAF funds to pay wages to charity workers, pay for fundraising activities, or pay for supplies for charities. The

---

[93] The provisions of the PPA place new restrictions on grants by DAFs and private foundations to non-functionally integrated Type III SOs.

[94] This information is necessary to determine whether a grant from a DAF to the organization may be a taxable distribution.

donor-advisor of one small DAF questioned how the DAF could continue to operate in a manner consistent with the purpose for which the fund was originally created in light of the PPA-enacted changes to section 4958 of the Code. An advocacy group and a group of DAF donor-advisors stressed that establishing a small public charity or private foundation instead of establishing a DAF would be cost-prohibitive for some individuals with small funds or modest programming goals. They argued that the net result of the PPA would be the loss to the public of beneficial programs.

Along these lines, many respondents were critical of a rule having the effect that DAF assets could no longer be used to pay for fundraising expenses, reimburse staff, fulfill existing pledges, or pay for the charitable portion of a bifurcated gift.[95] Those taking this position stressed that bifurcated gifts lead to new giving and thus benefited both the donor and charity and should therefore be permitted.

Finally, some respondents observed that the new PPA rules are leading to a reassessment by some donors as to which charitable vehicle they should choose. Specifically, some donors who might have opened a DAF are now choosing to operate a small, public charity instead.

Proposals from Respondents

The respondents to the request for public comments sometimes made policy proposals or recommendations for further study. Some of these include:

- **Payout requirements for NDAFs.** Regulate NDAFs instead of, or to a greater degree than, community foundations that sponsor DAFs.

  One respondent advocated a larger payout requirement for NDAFs to counter the structural incentive to keep assets under the management of their related financial institutions.

  An advocacy group that is critical of DAFs in general (and which favors treating nearly all DAFs like private foundations) encouraged the IRS to take a separate look at the "traditional DAF sponsors" and potentially exempt some of them from a more restrictive regulatory regime.

- **Charitable contribution deduction.** Reduce the donor's deduction for charitable contributions in particular circumstances.

  A state bar association proposed making the deductibility rules now applicable to gifts to private foundations applicable as well to DAFs and non-functionally integrated Type III SOs in order to be consistent with tax policy that favors putting assets to immediate charitable use.

  A contrasting view from a different respondent held that the deductibility rules are appropriate provided that the charitable assets were not hoarded indefinitely.

- **Donor control of assets.** Establish objective tests for control of assets.

---

[95] An example of a bifurcated gift is a fundraising dinner. Suppose the price to attend is $100 and the cost of the meal is $25. A charitable contribution deduction of only $75 is allowed because the attendee received a benefit of $25 (the meal).

A state bar association recommended minimum distribution requirements, prohibitions on retention of options or other rights, limits on management fees, a limited duration for advisory rights, and a limit on the lifetime of the DAF.

One respondent suggested the possibility of delaying the donor's deduction in the case where the donor has a right of first refusal to repurchase the property upon resale. The deduction would be available at the time the property is repurchased or the right of first refusal lapses.

- **Transfer of appreciated assets or illiquid property.**

One respondent suggested a possible formula requiring a percentage payout after a reasonable period of time to ensure the asset is sold. The formula would take into account factors such as asset type and marketability.

Another respondent proposed establishing best practices for sponsoring organizations that receive illiquid property. These would include a requirement that the donor provide an appraisal of the property. The appraisal would have to state that there is a market for the property and that it can be sold in a timely way. All encumbrances would also have to be disclosed or discharged except in usual cases, and carrying costs would have to be disclosed. The charity would be responsible for disposing of non-income producing properties within a reasonable period.

Overall, the public comments included a wide range of opinions on issues faced by DAFs and their sponsoring organizations as well as SOs and their supported organizations. They provided details of behaviors that donors and these entities engage in and how the PPA is likely to affect them. The comments inform Treasury's answers to the questions Congress posed, answers which are contained in the next chapter.

Chapter 5: Answering Congressional Questions

The broad issues of the relationships among charities and their donors, charitable contribution deductions, distribution requirements, and completed gifts, have been raised with respect to SOs and DAFs in recent years. These issues are important because an increasing amount of charitable dollars flow through SOs and DAFs. Data from Form 990 returns indicate that in 2006, SOs received $94.1 billion in revenue, had total expenses of $72.5 billion—including $11.5 billion in grants, $4.0 billion in payments to affiliates, and $46.9 billion in program expenses—and a net worth of $226.7 billion at the end of 2006. In addition, in 2006, *organizations* that sponsored DAFs received $59.5 billion in revenue, including $9.0 billion in contributions to DAFs. These sponsoring organizations had total expenses of $37.7 billion—including $5.7 billion in grants paid from DAF assets, $6.8 billion in other grants paid, and $20.7 billion in program expenses—and a net worth of $211.3 billion. At the end of 2006, the 2,398 organizations that sponsored DAFs reported having 160,000 individual DAFs with a total value of $31.1 billion.

DAFs, SOs, and small, private foundations may be considered alternative ways to structure giving by a donor interested solely in making grants to other charities. The permitted level of donor influence or control over the donated assets differs across the three types of entities. Contributions to a DAF, an SO, or a private foundation become the property of the respective entity and thus may qualify for charitable contribution deductions. In the case of a DAF, the donor has an advisory role in how the assets are invested and/or distributed, but the ultimate decision about how those assets are invested and distributed rests with the sponsoring organization, which generally is not controlled by the donor. In the case of an SO, the donor may have influence over the SO as a director, officer, or trustee of the SO, but the donor may not control the SO or its assets. In contrast, if a donor contributes assets to a private foundation (which may have been established by the donor), the donor may retain some influence over the use of the assets because the donor may have control of the private foundation.

Because of concerns that donors to some SOs and DAFs may be exercising undue influence over the donee organizations or the contributed assets, the PPA enacted several provisions specifically aimed at SOs and DAF sponsoring organizations. The PPA enacted additional disclosure and reporting requirements for both SOs and DAF sponsoring organizations, which increase the transparency of these organizations and enable more oversight by state and federal regulators, supported organizations, and the public. The PPA also enacted a set of excise taxes designed to ensure that the distributions from a DAF further a charitable purpose and do not result in inappropriate benefits to donors or their advisors. The excise taxes are levied on the sponsoring organization or approving managers. The PPA further enacted excise taxes on certain payments from a DAF or an SO to a donor (or a related person). The PPA also required a DAF donor to obtain a contemporaneous written acknowledgment from the sponsoring organization that the organization has exclusive legal control over the contributed assets. Finally, the PPA tightened the rules applicable to Type III SOs, which are not controlled by their supported organizations, and imposed the private foundation excess business holdings rules on DAFs and certain SOs.

Congress requested that Treasury consider four questions related to DAFs and SOs. Each is addressed in turn below.

Charitable Contribution Deduction

As noted above, SOs and DAFs may be used by donors as alternatives for small, private foundations if donors are willing to trade control of the organization for more generous charitable contribution deduction rules. Because of the public charity status of DAF sponsoring organizations and SOs, donors may be able to claim larger charitable contribution deductions, especially for gifts of appreciated property, and may deduct a greater portion of their income than if they donated to private foundations. Congress asked if the contribution deduction rules for SOs and DAFs are appropriate, giving consideration to the type, extent, and timing of the use of the donated assets. Congress also asked if these rules are appropriate, giving consideration to the use of the assets of DAFs and SOs for the benefit of the person making the charitable contribution or a related person. These two questions are addressed in turn below.

Although donors may prefer making gifts of appreciated property to SOs and DAFs, rather than to private foundations, in order to take a larger charitable contribution deduction, they may do so only if they are willing not only to part with control of the asset, but also to give the assets to organizations they generally do not control. As discussed above, private foundation donors often control the governing board of the foundation and thus may retain some indirect control of assets contributed to the foundation. This is not the case for DAFs and SOs. Donations to a DAF or an SO are owned by the sponsoring organization of the DAF or by the SO, which, like other public charities, is generally accountable to the public (either directly or, in the case of SOs, indirectly through their relationships with their supported organizations). Donors are expressly prohibited from controlling SOs and typically do not control DAF sponsoring organizations. Further, the PPA enacted reforms designed to mitigate undue donor influence on SOs and DAF sponsoring organizations. Because donors to DAFs and SOs are like donors to other public charities, giving up both control of the contributed assets and the ability to control the donee organization, the deduction rules seem appropriate.

To address perceived abuses involving non-cash contributions, the PPA enacted provisions with the purpose of strengthening the rules relating to gifts of property. These provisions apply equally to DAF sponsoring organizations and SOs as they do to other public charities.[96] Thus, the charitable deduction rules for gifts to DAFs and SOs, which are the same as the rules for gifts to other public charities, appear to be appropriate.

With respect to the timing of the use of charitable contributions, assets may be used to build or maintain an endowment, which generates a lag—sometimes years—between when the assets are donated—and a charitable contribution may be claimed—and when they are used to provide direct charitable services. Congress is interested in whether it is appropriate to allow a deduction today for contributions which will be used to meet charitable needs in the future. Although endowments can serve a positive role in the provision of charitable services,[97] preservation of an

---

[96] See, for example, section 1215 of the PPA (relating to the recapture of the tax benefit for charitable contributions of exempt use property not used for an exempt use) and section 1217 of the PPA (extending the time for charities to report dispositions of contributed property from two to three years).

[97] For example, endowments provide liquidity available for emergency projects, just like cash and liquid investments serve for for-profit organizations. Additionally, endowments allow for the smoothing of charitable expenditures over the business cycle. Finally, endowments can be used to provide for things that are not conducive to normal

endowment *as a goal* can lead the charity to drift over time from its charitable purpose or the donor's original intent. However, most issues relating to the timing of charitable deductions and use of donated assets are no different for SOs and DAF sponsoring organizations than they are for any other charitable organization, although reporting requirements differ across the types of charitable organizations. It is appropriate that the contribution rules for SOs and DAF sponsoring organizations are the same as those applicable to other public charities.

Several current provisions of the Code address issues related to donor benefits. A charitable deduction for a contribution to any public charity, including a DAF sponsoring organization or SO, is never appropriate to the extent that the donor or an associated individual or entity receives benefits in exchange for the contribution. A donor that claims a charitable contribution deduction for the full amount of such a contribution without accounting for the value of what was received in return is violating current law. This is an appropriate limitation on the charitable deduction in cases where an exchange of benefits, rather than a gift, takes place.

In addition, an organization's charitable status may be forfeited if it operates to benefit private interests, such as those of its donors. Further, section 4958 of the Code provides for excise taxes both on a donor who receives excess benefits from a public charity and on the charity's managers if they knowingly approved the transaction conferring the benefit. In addition, the PPA enacted new provisions designed to tax SOs, DAF sponsoring organizations, and their donors if donors receive certain payments or any improper benefits from an SO or DAF. These excise tax provisions are designed to deter the private use of the assets of public charities, including those held in DAFs and SOs, by donors and others.

Distribution Requirements

Private foundations, which are similar along some dimensions to DAFs, are required to distribute five percent of their non-exempt-use assets annually. DAF sponsoring organizations have no distribution requirements for DAF assets, either individually or in the aggregate. Congress asked if DAFs should have a distribution requirement.

IRS data indicate the average payout rate for Aggregate DAFs in 2006 was 9.3 percent of assets. Community foundation-sponsored Aggregate DAFs had an average payout rate that matched the overall average. Commercial NDAFs had an average payout rate of 14.2 percent (14.7 percent at the median). Other NDAFs had an average payout rate of 28.7 percent (10.5 percent at the median). The payout rates for private foundations tend to hover just above five percent. Thus, compared to private foundations, the average payout rates for Aggregate DAFs in 2006 appear to be high for most categories of DAF sponsoring organizations.[98] However, it would be premature

---

fundraising, e.g., capital projects such as upgrading outdated heating, plumbing or wiring systems or an expansion of a soup kitchen.

[98] This is relative to the roughly five percent payout rate observed for private non-operating foundations. However, again note that while these percentages provide some perspective on payout policy and practice, payout rates for DAFs and private foundations are not directly comparable. There are differences in the definitions of qualified expenditures, distributions, and assets reported by DAF sponsoring organizations and private foundations, which affect calculations of payout rates.

to make a recommendation regarding distribution requirements for DAFs on the basis of this first year of reported data.

These data come from new questions on Form 990 that require DAF sponsoring organizations to report the total number of DAFs, the aggregate value of assets held in those DAFs at year-end, and the aggregate contributions to and grants from those DAFs during the year. The new data will allow for calculation of aggregate payout rates, monitoring of certain trends related to DAFs, and comparison of payout rates for Aggregate DAFs with those of private foundations. Beginning with tax year 2008, the redesigned Form 990 asks for DAF-related information in a separate section. This will further improve the data available for analysis, including analysis of Aggregate DAF payout rates over time.

Individual DAF information is not collected, thus limiting the conclusions that may be drawn regarding activity levels in individual DAFs. Individual DAF payout rates may vary widely, and Aggregate DAF payout rates may mask low payout rates (or even no payout) from a subset of individual DAFs.

Donor Advice and Completed Gifts

A charitable gift is not considered to be "complete"—and no charitable deduction is allowed—if the donor maintains control over the gift, its sale, or its further use. Congress asked if having an advisory relationship in how funds are invested and/or distributed in the case of a DAF or an SO is consistent with a completed gift.

Contributions to DAFs and SOs are irrevocable and non-refundable (assuming that all existing tax and other legal requirements are met). Provided that the DAF sponsoring organization or the SO asserts contemporaneously that it holds all rights to contributed assets, the sponsoring organization or the SO—not the donor—is the legal owner of the contributed assets and controls how those assets are invested and disbursed. A donor's non-binding advisory relationship does not alter this legal relationship. Thus, just as a donor's control of a private foundation does not alter the fact that a gift to the foundation is complete, it is consistent to treat donations to DAFs and SOs that comply with existing legal requirements as completed gifts even if the donor retains non-binding advisory rights.

Donee organizations may feel pressure from donors to use donated funds in a manner preferred by the donor, especially when subsequent contributions may be desired. In this regard, however, there is nothing unique about the institutional structure of DAFs or SOs. Where donors have a close relationship to a donee organization, or where a small number of actors is involved—as is the case with many charities, including some SOs and DAF sponsoring organizations—this pressure may be exacerbated. Current law disallows a charitable contribution deduction for a contribution to any charity that does not meet the standard of a completed gift, including in the case of a gift to a DAF or SO.

Other Forms of Charity

Congress asked whether the issues described in questions 1-3 are also issues with respect to other forms of charities or charitable donations.

As noted above, issues relating to type, extent and timing of the use of charitable contributions, and the appropriateness of the existing charitable contribution rules, are the same for all public charities. Similarly, issues relating to when a charitable gift is considered complete are common to all charitable organizations.

Conclusion

The PPA enacted provisions designed to mitigate undue donor influence on SOs and DAF sponsoring organizations and to increase the required transparency of these organizations. New reporting requirements will make more data available to federal and state regulators, as well as to researchers, the press, and the general public. As the effects of the PPA and new regulations become clearer over time, Treasury looks forward to working with Congress to determine whether additional legislation or reporting is necessary.

Appendix A: Selected Bibliography

Barton, Noelle, 2008. "How the Chronicle's Annual Survey of Donor-Advised Funds Was Compiled." *The Chronicle of Philanthropy* 20.

Barton, Noelle, and Elizabeth Schwinn, 2008. "Growing Concerns and Assets: Donor-Advised Funds Gain in Popularity as Economy Softens." *The Chronicle of Philanthropy* 20.

Barton, Noelle, and Elizabeth Schwinn, 2007. "Modest Gains in Giving: Donations to Large Charities rose 4.3% in 2006." *The Chronicle of Philanthropy* 20.

Barton, Noelle, and Peter Panepento, 2007. "A Surge in Assets: Donor-Advised Funds are Growing Exponentially." *The Chronicle of Philanthropy* 19.

Bassett, Curtis R., 1993. "Supporting Organizations: Private Partnerships with Public Charity." *Trusts and Estates*.

Bier, Rivka, and Sharon M. Urban, 2006. "Being Charitable – Without Going Broke." *Tax Advisor*.

Bjorklund, Victoria B., 2000. "Charitable Giving to a Private Foundation: The Alternatives, the Supporting Organization, and the Donor-Advised Fund." 27 *The Exempt Organization Tax Review* 107.

Bjorklund, Victoria B., 2010. "Choosing Among the Private Foundation, Supporting Organization and Donor-Advised Fund, May 2003." Simpson Thacher & Bartlett, LLP. Available at http://www.stblaw.com/content/Publications/pub239.pdf. (Last accessed December 1, 2011.)

Bjorklund, Victoria B., 1998. "The Emergence of the Donor-Advised Fund." Paul *Streckfus' EO Tax Journal* 15 (3).

Bjorklund, Victoria B., 1998. "The Emergence of the Donor-Advised Fund." *Paul Streckfus' EO Tax Journal* 3.

Blattmachr, Jonathan G., 1993. "Tax and Nontax Advantages of Community Foundations." *Trusts and Estates*.

Blum, Debra, 2002. "Companies Compete on Donor Funds." *The Chronicle of Philanthropy* 14.

Breitstein, Joel, 2002. "Donor Advised Funds: A Good Vehicle for Charitable Planning." *Estate Planning* at 37.

Brody, Evelyn, 2005. "The Charity in Bankruptcy and Ghosts of Donors Past, Present, and Future." *Seton Hall Legislative Journal* 471 (29).

Brown, L. David., and Archana Kalegaonkar, 2002. "Support Organizations and the Evolution of the NGO Sector." *Nonprofit & Voluntary Sector Quarterly* 231 (31).

Brown, Susan D., and Antonia M. Grumbach, 1994. "Creative Planning Opportunities with Section 509(a)(3) Organizations--A Flexible Organizational Tool." New York University Twenty-Second Conference on Tax Planning for 501(c)(3) Organizations.

Committee on Community Foundations Legal Advisory Subcommittee, 1996. "Guide to Donor Involvement: Basic Considerations and Best Practices – A Resource for Community Foundations." Council on Foundations.

Darabi, L., 2006. "Alms Talks." *Institutional Investor*.

DeMent, Daniel L., 1992. "Majority Shareholders, Charitable Contributions and Community Foundations." *Private Foundations*.

DiRusso, Alyssa A., 2006. "Supporting the Supporting Organization: The Potential and Exploitation of 509(a)(3) Charities." *Indiana Law Review* 207(39).

Eason, John K., 2005. "Private Motive and Perpetual Conditions in Charitable Naming Gifts: When Good Names Go Bad." *U.C. Davis Law Review* 375(38).

Eiseman, Cynthia J., 1997. "Value Added: Donor-Advised Funds at Community Foundations." *Trusts and Estates* 16.

Everson. Mark W., 2005. "Written Statement of Mark W. Everson, Commissioner of Internal Revenue, Hearing on Charities and Charitable Giving: Proposals for Reform." April 5, 2005. U.S. Senate, Committee of Finance, Washington, DC. Available at http://finance.senate.gov/imo/media/doc/metest040505.pdf. (Last accessed December 1, 2011.)

Fahmy, Dalia, 2004. "Adventures in Philanthropy." *Institutional Investor*.

Fremont-Smith, Marion R., 2005. "*Is* It Time to Treat Private Foundations and Public Charities Alike?" 52 *The Exempt Organization Tax Review* 257.

Graddy, Elizabeth A., and Donald L. Morgan, 2006. "Community Foundations, Organizational Strategy, and Public Policy." *Nonprofit & Voluntary Sector Quarterly* 605(35).

Gravelle, Jane G., 2005. "Statement of Jane G. Gravelle, Senior Specialist in Economic Policy, Congressional Research Service, Hearing on Charities and Charitable Giving: Proposals for Reform." April 5, 2005. U.S. Senate, Committee of Finance, Washington, DC. Available at http://finance.senate.gov/imo/media/doc/jgtest040505.pdf. (Last accessed December 1, 2011.)

Hoyt, Christopher R., 1996. "Legal Compendium for Community Foundations."

Jones, Darryll K., 2001. "Regulating Donor Advised Funds." *Florida Bar Journal* 38.

Kerkman, Leah, and et al., 2005. "Growing Assets and Concerns: Proposed Rules Could Hurt Popularity of Advised Funds." *The Chronicle of Philanthropy* 17.

Kerkman, Leah, and et al., 2006. "A Soaring Year." *The Chronicle of Philanthropy* 18.

King, Stephen H., 1998. "Getting to the Heart of IRS Concerns with Donor-Designated Giving." *Journal of Taxation of Exempt Organizations*.

Klausner, Michael, 2003. "When Time Isn't Money: Foundation Payouts and the Time Value of Money." 41 *The Exempt Organization Tax Review* 421.

Korman, Rochelle, and William F. Gaske, 1994. "Supporting Organizations to Community Foundations: A Little-Used Alternative to Private Foundations." 10 *The Exempt Organization Tax Review* 1327 .

Larose, Marni D., and Brad Wolverton, 2003. "Donor Advised Funds Experience Drop in Contributions, Survey Finds." *The Chronicle of Philanthropy* 15.

Leibell, David T., and Daniel L. Daniels, 2005. "Target: Supporting Organizations." *Trusts and Estates*.

Leibell, David T., and Daniel L. Daniels, 2006. "Venture Philanthropy on a Roll." *Trusts and Estates*.

Ostrander, Susan A., 2007. "Ostrander's Reply to Schervish," *Nonprofit & Voluntary Sector Quarterly* 380(36).

Ostrander, Susan A., 2007. "The Growth of Donor Control: Revisiting the Social Relations of Philanthropy." *Nonprofit & Voluntary Sector Quarterly* 356 (36).

Park, Benetta Y., 2000. "Supporting Organization: New Reigning Charitable Entity." *Trusts and Estates*.

Rodriguez, Albert R., and et al., 1997. "The Tax-Exempt Status of Commercially-Sponsored Donor-Advised Funds." 17 *The Exempt Organization Tax Review* 95.

Rothschild, Alan F., Jr., 2004. "How Donors May and May Not Exercise Control of Charitable Gifts." 16 *Journal of Taxation of Exempt Organizations* 16 (110).

Schervish, Paul G., 2007. "Is Today's Philanthropy Failing Beneficiaries? Always a Risk, But Not for the Most Part." *Nonprofit & Voluntary Sector Quarterly* 373(36).

Schlesinger, S.J., and M.R. Goodman, 2004. "Supporting Organizations: An Antidote to Lack of Public Funding." 31 *Estate Planning* 398.

Shevlin, David A., 2003. "Recent Court Decisions Highlight the Complexity of the Rules Governing 'Type 3' Supporting Organizations." *The Exempt Organization Tax Review*.

Shevlin, David A., 2001. "Donor-Advised Funds: The Applicability of Rule 12b-1 Fees and Trail Commissions." *The Exempt Organization Tax Review*.

Steuerle, Eugene, 1999. "Charitable Endowments, Advised Funds and the Mutual Fund Industry, Part 1." *Tax Notes* 129(82).

Steuerle, Eugene, 1999. "Charitable Endowments, Advised Funds and the Mutual Fund Industry, Part 2." *Tax Notes* 257(82).

Steuerle, Eugene, 2007. "A Method for Measuring and Partially Testing 'Charitability.'" *Tax Notes* 489 (116).

Teitell, Conrad, 2004. "Public Charities, Advised Funds, Supporting Organizations and Foundations: Selecting Wisely." In 2004 *National Committee on Planned Giving Conference Proceedings*, 805.

Treacy, Gerald B., Jr., 2006. "What's Left of SOs?" *Trusts and Estates*.

Treacy, Gerald B., Jr., 2007. "Cold Snap for DAFs." *Trusts and Estates*.

Ugolini, Joel, 2003. "The Difficulties of Establishing a Supporting Organization When Making Charitable Contributions to a Donor-Advised Fund Program: Lapham Foundation Inc. v. Commissioner." *The Tax Lawyer* 56(4).

U.S. Government Accountability Office, 2010. "Tax-Exempt Organizations: Collecting More Data on Donor-Advised Funds and Supporting Organizations Could Help Address Compliance Challenges (2006)." Washington, DC. Available at http://www.gao.gov/new.items/d06799.pdf. (Last accessed December 1, 2011.)

Weber, Fredrick B., 2001. "Supporting Organizations: The Less Expensive Alternative to Private Foundations." *Illinois Bar Journal* 128(89).

Wolverton, Brad, 2003. "Surviving Tough Times: Big Charities Suffer First Drop in Donations in 12 Years." *The Chronicle of Philanthropy 16*.

Appendix B: Congressional Mandate

Section 1226 of the PPA is titled "Study on Donor Advised Funds and Supporting Organizations." The text of this section[99] is as follows:

> (a) STUDY.—The Secretary of the Treasury shall undertake a study on the organization and operation of donor advised funds (as defined in section 4966(d)(2) of the Internal Revenue Code of 1986, as added by this Act) and of organizations described in section 509(a)(3) of such Code. The study shall specifically consider—
>> (1) whether the deductions allowed for the income, gift, or estate taxes for charitable contributions to sponsoring organizations (as defined in section 4966(d)(1) of such Code, as added by this Act) of donor advised funds or to organizations described in section 509(a)(3) of such Code are appropriate in consideration of—
>>> (A) the use of contributed assets (including the type, extent, and timing of such use), or
>>> (B) the use of the assets of such organizations for the benefit of the person making the charitable contribution (or a person related to such person),
>> (2) whether donor advised funds should be required to distribute for charitable purposes a specified amount (whether based on the income or assets of the fund) in order to ensure that the sponsoring organization with respect to such donor advised fund is operating consistent with the purposes or functions constituting the basis for its exemption under section 501, or its status as an organization described in section 509(a), of such Code,
>> (3) whether the retention by donors to organizations described in paragraph (1) of rights or privileges with respect to amounts transferred to such organizations (including advisory rights or privileges with respect to the making of grants or the investment of assets) is consistent with the treatment of such transfers as completed gifts that qualify for a deduction for income, gift, or estate taxes, and
>> (4) whether the issues raised by paragraphs (1), (2), and (3) are also issues with respect to other forms of charities or charitable donations.
> (b) REPORT.—Not later than 1 year after the date of the enactment of this Act, the Secretary of the Treasury shall submit to the Committee on Finance of the Senate and the Committee on Ways and Means of the House of Representatives a report on the study conducted under subsection (a) and make such recommendations as the Secretary of the Treasury considers appropriate.

---

[99] The text can be found on page 1,094 of http://frwebgate.access.gpo.gov/cgi-bin/getdoc.cgi?dbname=109_cong_public_laws&docid=f:publ280.109.pdf. (Last accessed December 1, 2011.)

Appendix C: Data Appendix

The primary source for the data on SOs and DAF sponsoring organizations that are analyzed in this report is the IRS Statistics of Income 2006 Form 990 file. This dataset is based on a stratified random sample that includes 100 percent of the largest charitable organizations and smaller percentages of smaller organizations. For this study, 2,154 sample observations reporting status as an SO were weighted to the population of 20,807 SOs using the sample weights. The population of 3,358 DAF sponsoring organizations was represented by 677 observations.

Because 2006 was the first year that many of the questions about DAFs and SOs were included on Form 990, it was not surprising that the information was reported incorrectly or not reported at all in many cases. Reporting errors present the issue of whether to report the original erroneous information or to make corrections when possible. For this report, to the extent possible, other sources of information, including the organization's 2007 return or web site, when available, were used to supply missing information or remedy obvious reporting or coding errors. It is likely that many errors remain in the reported data, however. The following discusses the primary situations where other data sources were used to supply missing information or make corrections and adjustments to the data.

Nearly 1,900 organizations checked the box on Schedule A as SOs but did not specify the type of SO. By checking the 2007 returns and the websites of these organizations, the type of SO could be determined in all but 288 cases. In addition, about 45 percent of the SOs did not report any dollar amount of support in response to the new questions on Schedule A. A significant number of these organizations reported on the first page of Form 990 that they had made payments to affiliated organizations. While this number would not include the value of any services to the supported organization, it was assumed that such payments would generally represent a lower bound for measuring support. Some other organizations reported the same dollar amount for support provided as for payments to affiliates, suggesting that in at least some cases, payments to affiliates is a good indication of the amount of support.

Reporting for DAFs was also incomplete or was incorrectly reported. Some organizations answered the question of whether they owned DAFs in the affirmative but did not report the number of individual DAFs or their value. A few organizations reported that they had one DAF when it was clear from other information on their website or later returns that they had many individual DAFs. It was unclear whether this was because the question was interpreted as if all of the individual DAFs were considered a single entity. Other reporting errors included putting the DAF information in the spaces for non-DAF advised accounts, putting the same numbers in both locations, and putting the dollar amount of the aggregate value at the end of the year in the spaces for the number of accounts.

Problems were also found in the reporting of contributions to DAFs and grants made from DAFs. Because this was the first year for separating DAF from non-DAF contributions, some organizations did not separate the amounts but instead reported all the information on either the DAF or non-DAF lines. In cases where the 2007 return indicated that they had both kinds of transactions, the amounts for 2006 were allocated based on the 2007 proportions or the percentages of DAF and non-DAF assets, where available. The new lines for reporting DAF information in 2006 were the first lines in the sections for revenues and expenses, which were previously the lines used to record total contributions and grants. A number of organizations continued to report their total contributions and grants on the first lines, incorrectly implying that they had received contributions to DAFs or made grants from DAFs. Where these organizations did not have other indications of DAFs, the amounts were transferred to the non-DAF lines. It was sometimes difficult to determine the most appropriate adjustments.

The table below shows the originally reported and final values for the primary DAF-related information on the 2006 Form 990. While the aggregate dollar values did not change greatly, adjustments and corrections were made to all variables for at least some returns. The numbers for returns not answering "yes" to whether they owned DAFs at the end of the year reflected cases where the question was not answered "yes," but other information showed that these organizations had DAFs.

Table C.1: Original Reported and Adjusted Values of DAF Information, Unweighted, 2006

| | | Own DAFs? | | NDAF | | Sector | | | Religious | |
DAF Variable	Total	No	Yes	Com-mercial	Other	Educa-tion	Community Foundations	Health	NEC	Other
Number of returns with:										
DAFs - reported	1,880	0	1,880	17	14	378	598	206	208	459
DAFs - adjusted	1,904	13	1,891	23	19	379	604	206	213	460
DAF value - reported	2,056	0	2,056	17	14	457	599	205	265	499
DAF value - adjusted	2,060	13	2,046	23	19	458	604	205	269	481
DAF contributions - reported	1,647	75	1,572	12	14	146	476	172	297	456
DAF contributions - adjusted	1,612	81	1,532	23	19	145	513	169	299	376
DAF grants - reported	1,135	92	1,042	15	8	70	428	130	277	135
DAF grants - adjusted	1,189	40	1,149	23	19	71	512	130	285	142
Total number of DAFs										
reported	6,998,363	0	6,998,363	60,153	9,066	12,843	6,824,855	1,266	20,323	69,857
adjusted	1,904	13	1,891	23	19	379	604	206	213	460
Dollar amounts (in millions)										
DAF value - reported	30,052	0	3,052	9,196	1,047	1,373	13,311	192	4,617	315
DAF value - adjusted	31,098	660	30,438	9,797	1,140	1,428	13,455	192	4,764	321
DAF contributions - reported	63	0	63	0	0	0	63	0	0	0
DAF contributions - adjusted	0	0	0	0	0	0	0	0	0	0
DAF grants - reported	3,033	3	3,030	215	4	108	2,296	30	350	29
DAF grants - adjusted	2,501	0	2,501	0	4	53	2,197	28	195	24

Notes: The total number of DAFs included one observation reporting the value of DAFs in the space for the number of accounts.

Source: IRS Statistics of Income, Form 990 File, 2006

Appendix D: Notice 2006-109

The text of Notice 2006-109 is found on page 1,121 of Internal Revenue Bulletin 2006-51 at http://www.irs.gov/pub/irs-irbs/irb06-51.pdf. (Last accessed December 1, 2011.)

Part III – Administrative, Procedural, and Miscellaneous

Interim Guidance Regarding Supporting Organizations and Donor Advised Funds

Notice 2006-109

Section 1. PURPOSE

This Notice provides interim guidance regarding the application of certain requirements enacted as part of the Pension Protection Act of 2006, Pub. L. No. 109-208, 120 Stat. 780 (2006) ("PPA"), that affect supporting organizations, donor advised funds, and private foundations that make grants to supporting organizations.

Sections 1231, 1241,1242, 1243, and 1244 of the PPA add sections 509(f), 4943(f), 4958(c)(3), 4966, and 4967, to the Internal Revenue Code ("Code"), and amend sections 509(a)(3)(B), 4942(g)(4), and 4945(d)(4)(A) of the Code. The amendments to section 509(a)(3) and the addition of section 509(f) prescribe new requirements for supporting organizations. The addition of section 4943(f) defines the terms "Type III supporting organization" and "functionally integrated Type III supporting organization."

The amendments to sections 4942 and 4945 affect private foundations that make grants or similar payments to supporting organizations under certain circumstances. The amendments to section 4958, among other things, subject substantial contributors and persons related to them (as described in section 4958(c)(3)(B)) to new excise taxes if they engage in certain types of transactions with supporting organizations with which they have a relationship. New section 4966 imposes an excise tax on a sponsoring organization that maintains donor advised funds if it makes certain distributions from a donor advised fund. New section 4967 imposes excise taxes on certain distributions from a donor advised fund that provide more than an incidental benefit to a donor, a donor-advisor, or related persons (as described in sections 4967(d) and 4958(f)(7)).

This notice provides guidance on four aspects of the application of these new provisions of the Code. First, Section 3 provides criteria for private foundations that might make distributions to supporting organizations that can be used to determine for purposes of sections 4942(g)(4) and 4945(d)(4) whether an organization is a Type I, Type II, or functionally integrated Type III supporting organization. Section 3 also provides criteria for determining whether a supporting organization, or any of its supported organizations, are controlled by disqualified persons. Section 3 also provides similar guidance with respect to section 4966 for donor advised funds that make grants to supporting organizations. Second, Section 4 clarifies the date of applicability for the new section 4958(c)(3) excise tax on certain excess benefit transactions involving supporting organizations. Third, pursuant to the authority under new section 4966(d)(2)(C), Section 5.01 excludes certain employer-sponsored disaster relief funds from the definition of

92

donor-advised fund. Fourth, Section 5.02 clarifies how the Internal Revenue Service ("Service") will apply the new section 4966(a) excise taxes with respect to payments made pursuant to educational grants awarded prior to the date of enactment of the PPA.

This notice is intended to address a limited number of issues which require immediate guidance. The Service and the Department of Treasury ("Treasury") expect to issue further guidance, including regulations, under these provisions of the PPA. The rules provided in this notice apply until further guidance is issued. This notice does not affect the substantive standards for tax exemption under section 501(c)(3). This notice also invites comments from the public regarding this notice and suggestions for future guidance implementing statutory changes under the PPA.

Section 2. BACKGROUND

Organizations that are organized and operated exclusively for charitable, religious, educational or other specified purposes are generally exempt from income tax under section 501(a) as organizations described in section 501(c)(3). Section 509(a) divides section 501(c)(3) organizations into two subcategories: private foundations and organizations that are not private foundations, which are commonly known as public charities. To be categorized as a public charity and not a private foundation, an organization must be described in section 509(a). To be described in section 509(a)(1) or (2), an organization must receive a substantial amount of public support to fund its operations. To be described in section 509(a)(3), an organization must have a particular type of structural relationship with a publicly supported section 501(c)(3), (4), (5) or (6) organization.

Private foundations are subject to a different regime of excise taxes than are public charities. For example, private foundations are subject to excise tax if they do not make at least a minimum level of qualifying distributions each year. Private foundations are also subject to excise tax if they make certain taxable expenditures. Taxable expenditures include, but are not limited to, certain grants to organizations unless the private foundation exercises expenditure responsibility with respect to the grants as required by section 4945(h) and Treas. Reg. section 53.4945-5(b).

Section 170(c) describes organizations eligible to receive charitable contributions that are deductible for income tax purposes.

.01 Donor Advised Funds and Supporting Organizations before the PPA

Donor Advised Funds

Prior to the PPA, the Code did not define the term donor advised fund. However, the term was commonly understood to refer to component funds of certain community trusts. See Treas. Reg. section 1.170A-9(e)(10) and (11). The term was also commonly understood to refer to an account established by one or more donors but owned and controlled by a public charity to which such donors or other individuals designated by the donors could provide nonbinding recommendations regarding distributions from the account or regarding investment of the assets in the account.

Supporting Organizations

Section 509(a)(3) excludes from the definition of private foundation certain organizations that support certain publicly supported organizations. The Treasury regulations under section 509(a)(3) refer to these organizations as supporting organizations. To be described in section 509(a)(3), an organization must meet several tests: (1) it must be organized and operated exclusively for the benefit of specified publicly supported organizations (generally, public charities); (2) it must have one of three types of relationships with its publicly supported organizations; and (3) it must not be controlled, directly or indirectly, by disqualified persons (as defined in section 4946 other than foundation managers) with respect to such supporting organization.

In general, supporting organizations have been identified by the type of relationship they have with their publicly supported organizations. A supporting organization that is operated, supervised or controlled by one or more publicly supported organizations is commonly known as a Type I supporting organization. A supporting organization supervised or controlled in connection with one or more publicly supported organizations is commonly known as a Type II supporting organization. A supporting organization that is operated in connection with one or more publicly supported organizations is commonly known as a Type III supporting organization.

.02 Donor Advised Funds Under the PPA

Definition of a Donor Advised Fund

Under new section 4966(d)(2), a donor advised fund is defined as a fund or account owned and controlled by a sponsoring organization, which is separately identified by reference to contributions of a donor or donors, and with respect to which the donor, or any person appointed or designated by such donor ("donor advisor"), has, or reasonably expects to have, advisory privileges with respect to the distribution or investment of the funds.

A sponsoring organization is defined under new section 4966(d)(1) as a section 170(c) organization that is not a governmental organization (referenced in section 170(c)(1) and (2)(A)) or a private foundation and maintains one or more donor advised funds.

Pursuant to new section 4966(d)(2)(B), the term donor advised fund does not include a fund or account: (1) that makes distributions only to a single identified organization or governmental entity or (2) with respect to which a donor advises a sponsoring organization regarding grants for travel, study or similar purposes if:
  (A) the donor's, or the donor advisor's, advisory privileges are performed in his capacity as a member of a committee whose members are appointed by the sponsoring organization,
  (B) no combination of donors or donor advisors (or related persons) directly or indirectly control the committee, and
  (C) all grants are awarded on an objective and nondiscriminatory basis pursuant to a procedure approved in advance by the sponsoring organization's board of directors.

Thus, a sponsoring organization that owns and controls a fund that meets these criteria may award a scholarship from the fund to a natural person without subjecting the sponsoring organization or its managers to excise taxes under new section 4966.

Taxable Distribution

New section 4966 imposes an excise tax on a sponsoring organization for each taxable distribution it makes from a donor advised fund. It also imposes an excise tax on the agreement of any fund manager of the sponsoring organization to the making of a distribution, knowing that it is a taxable distribution. The tax on taxable distributions applies to distributions occurring in taxable years beginning after August 17, 2006.

In general, under new section 4966(c), a taxable distribution is any distribution from a donor advised fund to any natural person, or to any other person if (i) the distribution is for any purpose other than one specified in section 170(c)(2)(B), or (ii) the sponsoring organization maintaining the donor advised fund does not exercise expenditure responsibility with respect to such distribution in accordance with section 4945(h).

Under new section 4966(c)(2), a taxable distribution does not include a distribution from a donor advised fund to: (1) any organization described in section 170(b)(1)(A) (other than a disqualified supporting organization), (2) the sponsoring organization of such donor advised fund, or (3) any other donor advised fund.

Under new section 4966(d)(4), a disqualified supporting organization includes a Type III supporting organization that is not functionally integrated and any Type I, Type II, or functionally integrated Type III supporting organization where the donor or donor advisor (and any related parties) directly or indirectly controls a supported organization of the supporting organization.

Prohibited Benefit

New section 4967 imposes an excise tax if a donor, donor advisor, or a person related to a donor or donor advisor of a donor advised fund (as described in sections 4967(d) and 4958(f)(7)) provides advice as to a distribution that results in any such person receiving, directly or indirectly, a more than incidental benefit. The excise tax is imposed on any person who advises as to the distribution or who receives the benefit. A separate excise tax may be imposed on a fund manager who agreed to the making of the distribution. The new excise tax under section 4967 applies to taxable years beginning after August 17, 2006.

Secretarial Authority

New section 4966(d)(2)(C) grants the Secretary authority to exempt certain funds from treatment as donor advised funds if either (1) the fund or account is advised by a committee not directly or indirectly controlled by the donor or donor advisor (and any related parties), or (2) such fund or account benefits a single identified charitable purpose.

.03 Supporting Organizations Under the PPA

Supporting Organization Definition

The PPA incorporates the previously informal nomenclature used to distinguish among types of supporting organizations into the statute. Thus, new section 4966(d)(4)(B)(i) defines a Type I supporting organization as a supporting organization that is operated, supervised, or controlled by one or more section 509(a)(1) or 509(a)(2) organizations. New section 4966(d)(4)(B)(ii) defines a Type II supporting organization as a supporting organization that is supervised or controlled in connection with one or more section 509(a)(1) or 509(a)(2) organizations. (See also sections 4942(g)(4)(B)(i) and (ii) for parallel definitions of Type I and Type II supporting organizations). Finally, new section 4943(f)(5)(A) defines a Type III supporting organization as a supporting organization that is operated in connection with a section 509(a)(1) or (2) organization.

New section 4943(f)(5)(B) defines a functionally integrated Type III supporting organization as one which is not required under regulations established by the Secretary to make payments to supported organizations due to the activities of the organization related to performing the functions of, or carrying out the purposes of, such supported organizations.

New section 509(f)(2), which is effective August 17, 2006, prohibits certain supporting organizations from accepting gifts or contributions from certain persons associated with the supported organization of such supporting organization. This provision provides that any organization that would otherwise meet the requirements of a Type I or Type III supporting organization will be excluded under this provision if it accepts any gift or contribution from a person who directly or indirectly controls (either alone or together with related persons described in section 509(f)(2)(B)(ii) and (iii)) the governing body of a supported organization of such supporting organization or from a related person described in section 509(f)(2)(B).

New Rules Regarding Section 4958 Excess Benefit Transactions and Supporting Organizations

Section 4958 imposes an excise tax on certain persons if they engage in one or more excess benefit transactions. New section 4958(c)(3) provides that any grant, loan, compensation, or other similar payment from a supporting organization to a substantial contributor or persons related to the substantial contributor (as described in section 4958(c)(3)(B)) is treated as an excess benefit transaction. In addition, any loan from a supporting organization to certain disqualified persons is treated as an excess benefit transaction. The entire amount of the payment to such persons constitutes an excess benefit subject to an excise tax under section 4958. This excise tax applies to transactions occurring after July 25, 2006.

Under new section 4958(c)(3)(C), a substantial contributor includes any person who contributed or bequeathed an aggregate amount of more than $5,000 to the organization, if such amount is more than 2 percent of the total contributions and bequests received by the organization before the close of the taxable year of the organization in which the contribution or bequest is received. A substantial contributor also includes the creator of a trust.

.04 New Restrictions on Grants Made by Private Foundations to Supporting Organizations

The PPA amended section 4942(g) to deny qualifying distribution treatment to grants by non-operating private foundations to (1) Type III supporting organizations that are not functionally integrated and (2) to Type I, Type II, and functionally integrated Type III supporting organizations if a disqualified person of the private foundation directly or indirectly controls such supporting organization or a supported organization of the supporting organization. The PPA also amended section 4945(d)(4)(A) to treat grants to the above entities by all private foundations as taxable expenditures unless the private foundation exercises expenditure responsibility with respect to the grants.

Section 3. GRANTOR RELIANCE STANDARDS FOR GRANTS TO CERTAIN SUPPORTING ORGANIZATIONS

.01 Treatment of Grants from Private Foundations or Donor Advised Funds to Supporting Organizations

As stated in Section 2.04, the enactment of the PPA imposes certain limitations if a private foundation makes a grant to (1) a Type III supporting organization that is not functionally integrated, or (2) a Type I, Type II, or functionally integrated Type III supporting organization if one or more disqualified persons of the private foundation directly or indirectly controls such supporting organization or one of its supported organizations. Specifically, for non-operating foundations, the grant is not a qualifying distribution under section 4942. For all private foundations, the grant is a taxable expenditure under section 4945 if the private foundation does not exercise expenditure responsibility with respect to the grant.

Similarly, the PPA treats as a taxable distribution any distribution from a donor advised fund to (1) a Type III supporting organization that is not functionally integrated, or (2) any other supporting organization if the fund's donor or donor advisor (and any related parties) directly or indirectly controls a supported organization of the grantee if the sponsoring organization does not exercise expenditure responsibility with respect to such distribution.

Until further guidance is issued, for purposes of sections 4942, 4945, and 4966 (as applicable) a grantor, acting in good faith, may rely on information from the IRS Business Master File ("BMF") or the grantee's current IRS letter recognizing the grantee as exempt from federal income tax and indicating the grantee's public charity classification in determining whether the grantee is a public charity under section 509(a)(1), (2), or (3). In addition, a grantor, acting in good faith, may rely on a written representation from a grantee and specified documents as described in A. and B. below in determining whether the grantee is a Type I, Type II, or functionally integrated Type III supporting organization. The good faith requirement is not satisfied if the collected specified documents are inconsistent with the written representation. In each case, the grantor must verify that the grantee is listed in Publication 78, *Cumulative List of Organizations described in Section 170(c) of the Internal Revenue Code of 1986*, or obtain a copy of the current IRS letter recognizing the grantee as exempt from federal income tax.

97

A. To establish that a grantee is a Type I or a Type II supporting organization, a grantor, acting in good faith, may rely on a written representation signed by an officer, director or trustee of the grantee that the grantee is a Type I or Type II supporting organization, provided that:
   i. the representation describes how the grantee's officers, directors, or trustees are selected, and references any provisions in governing documents that establish a Type I (operated, supervised, or controlled by) or a Type II (supervised or controlled in connection with) relationship (as applicable) between the grantee and its supported organization(s); and
   ii. the grantor collects and reviews copies of governing documents of the grantee (and, if relevant, of the supported organization(s)).
B. To establish that a grantee is a functionally integrated Type III supporting organization a grantor, acting in good faith, may rely on a written representation signed by an officer, director or trustee of the grantee that the grantee is a functionally integrated Type III supporting organization, provided that:
   i. the grantee's representation identifies the one or more supported organizations with which the grantee is functionally integrated;
   ii. the grantor collects and reviews copies of governing documents of the grantee (and, if relevant, of the supported organization(s)), and any other documents that set forth the relationship of the grantee to its supported organizations, if such relationship is not reflected in the governing documents; and
   iii. the grantor collects and reviews a written representation signed by an officer, director or trustee of each of the supported organizations with which the grantee represents that it is functionally integrated describing the activities of the grantee and confirming, consistent with Section 3.02 of this notice, that but for the involvement of the grantee engaging in activities to perform the functions of, or to carry out the purposes of, the supported organization, the supported organization would normally be engaged in those activities itself.

As an alternative to relying on a written representation from a grantee and specified documents as described in A. or B. above, a grantor may rely on a reasoned written opinion of counsel of either the grantor or the grantee concluding that the grantee is a Type I, Type II, or functionally integrated Type III supporting organization.

A private foundation considering a grant to a Type I, Type II, or functionally integrated Type III supporting organization may need to obtain a list of the grantee's supported organizations from the grantee to determine whether any of the supported organizations is controlled by disqualified persons of the private foundation. See Section 3.02, below, for the definition of control that may be used. If such control exists, the grant may not be a qualifying distribution and the foundation may be required to exercise expenditure responsibility with respect to the grant.

Similarly, a sponsoring organization considering a grant from a donor advised fund to a Type I, Type II, or functionally integrated Type III supporting organization may need to obtain a list of the grantee's supported organizations from the grantee to determine whether any of the supported organizations is controlled by the fund's donor or donor advisor (and any related parties). <u>See</u> Section 3.02, below, for the definition of control that may be used. If such control exists, the sponsoring organization will be required to exercise expenditure responsibility.

.02 Standards for Determining Control and for Defining "Functionally Integrated Type III Supporting Organization"

The Service and the Treasury Department intend to issue regulations regarding the meaning of "control" under sections 4942(g)(4)(A) and 4966(d)(4)(A) and the definition of a "functionally integrated Type III supporting organization" under section 4943(f)(5)(B). Until those regulations are issued, a grantor may rely on the standards described below for purposes of sections 4942, 4945 and 4966 (as applicable). Although regulations may adopt different standards from those referenced below, those regulations will apply to grants made by private foundations and sponsoring organizations no sooner than the date that the regulations are proposed. The standards set forth below will apply with respect to any grants made prior to that date.

In determining whether a disqualified person with respect to a private foundation controls a supporting organization or one of its supported organizations, the control standards established in Treas. Reg. section 53.4942(a)-3(a)(3) will apply. Under these standards, an organization is controlled by one or more disqualified persons with respect to a foundation if any such persons may, by aggregating their votes or positions of authority, require the supporting or supported organization to make an expenditure, or prevent the supporting organization or the supported organization from making an expenditure, regardless of the method by which the control is exercised or exercisable.

Similarly, in determining whether a donor or donor advisor or a person related to a donor or donor advisor (as described in sections 4967(d) and 4958(f)(7)) of any donor advised fund controls a supported organization of the grantee, the control standards established in Treas. Reg. section 53.4942(a)-3(a)(3) will apply. Under these standards, a supported organization is controlled by one or more donor or donor advisors (and any related parties) of any donor advised fund if any such persons may, by aggregating their votes or positions of authority, require a supported organization to make an expenditure, or prevent a supported organization from making an expenditure, regardless of the method by which the control is exercised or exercisable.

Also, solely for purposes of a representation or opinion of counsel on which a grantor may rely, an organization will be considered a functionally integrated Type III supporting organization if it would meet the test set forth in Treas. Reg. section 1.509(a)-4(i)(3)(ii).

Section 4. APPLICABILITY DATE FOR EXCESS BENEFIT TRANSACTIONS BY SUPPORTING ORGANIZATIONS

As stated in Section 2.03, under section 4958(c), as amended by the PPA, any grant, loan, compensation, or other similar payment by a supporting organization to a substantial contributor or a person related to a substantial contributor (as described in section 4958(c)(3)(B)), and any loan provided by a supporting organization to certain disqualified persons, is treated automatically as an excess benefit transaction, with the entire amount paid to the substantial contributor or disqualified person and those related to them treated as an excess benefit. The statute provides that this new rule applies to transactions occurring after July 25, 2006.

Treasury and the IRS understand that before the PPA was enacted on August 17, 2006, a supporting organization may have entered into a binding contract or other legal obligation to pay substantial contributors, or persons related to substantial contributors, for goods or services, or to provide a loan to a disqualified person. At the time the supporting organization entered into these contracts or other legal obligations, the payments required under them were not necessarily considered excess benefit transactions.

To address the change to the law under the PPA, the IRS will not consider any payment made pursuant to a written contract that was binding on August 17, 2006 as an excess benefit transaction under new section 4958(c)(3), provided that (1) such contract was binding at all times after August 17, 2006 and before payment is made, (2) the contract is not modified during such period, and (3) the payment under the contract is made on or before August 17, 2007. Termination of the contract does not constitute a modification for this purpose.

Similarly, relief is provided with respect to certain arrangements that are not governed by a binding written contract described in the preceding paragraph. With respect to any such arrangement involving an employment relationship in existence, or other legal obligation in effect, on August 17, 2006, the IRS will not consider any payment pursuant to such an arrangement as an excess benefit transaction under new section 4958(c)(3), provided that (1) the terms of such arrangement are not modified after August 17, 2006, (2) any services are performed and any goods are delivered as required by the arrangement no later than December 31, 2006, and (3) the payment is made no later than August 17, 2007. Termination of the arrangement does not constitute a modification for this purpose.

The applicability dates set forth in this section affect only liability for excise taxes under new section 4958(c)(3). Notwithstanding any relief provided in this section, if the supporting organization pays in excess of reasonable compensation for services or in excess of fair market value for goods, it jeopardizes continued tax exemption under section 501(c)(3), and the individuals receiving the payments may be subject to excise taxes under section 4958. In addition, any relief provided by this section does not alter whether a transaction is an excess benefit transaction under section 4958(c)(1).

Section 5. DONOR ADVISED FUNDS

New section 4966(c)(1)(A) imposes an excise tax on all distributions to natural persons from donor advised funds effective for taxable years beginning after August 17, 2006. However, pursuant to the authority described in Section 2.02 above, certain funds or accounts are excepted from the definition of donor advised fund.

.01 Employer-Sponsored Disaster Relief Assistance Programs

The definition of donor advised fund in section 4966(d)(2)(A) encompasses all funds and accounts owned or controlled by a sponsoring organization separately identified with reference to the contribution of a donor or donors for which the donor, or anyone appointed by the donor, has or reasonably expects to have, advisory privileges. Section 4966(d)(2)(C) grants the Secretary the authority to exempt a fund or account (a "fund") from the definition of donor advised fund.

Certain employers may establish disaster relief funds at a community foundation or other public charity to provide disaster relief grants to employees or their family members who are the victims of a major disaster. The sponsoring organization may receive contributions to these funds from both the employer and its employees. If these employer-sponsored disaster relief funds are within the definition of donor advised funds, any distribution from these funds to employees or their family members would be subject to excise tax under new section 4966.

Pursuant to the authority under 4966(d)(2)(C), the IRS and Department of Treasury exclude from the definition of donor advised fund any employer-sponsored disaster relief fund that meets the following requirements:
  a. the fund serves a single identified charitable purpose, which is to provide relief from one or more qualified disasters within the meaning of section 139(c)(1), (2), or (3);[100]
  b. the fund serves a large or indefinite class (a "charitable class");
  c. recipients of grants from the fund are selected based on objective determinations of need;
  d. the selection of recipients of grants from the fund is made using either an independent selection committee or adequate substitute procedures to ensure that any benefit to the employer is incidental and tenuous. The selection committee is independent if a majority of the members of the committee consists of persons who are not in a position to exercise substantial influence over the affairs of the employer;
  e. no payment is made from the fund to or for the benefit of
    i.   any director, officer, or trustee of the sponsoring organization of the fund, or
    ii. members of the fund's selection committee; and
  f. the fund maintains adequate records that demonstrate the recipients' needs for the disaster relief assistance provided.

Satisfaction of these requirements does not affect the determination of whether any payments made from the fund might result in taxable compensation to the employees.

.02 Applicability Date for Educational Grants

As provided in Section 2.02 above, under new section 4966, distributions to natural persons from a donor advised fund are subject to an excise tax. The PPA provides that section 4966 applies to certain distributions (including certain educational grants) made in taxable years beginning after

---

[100] Under sections 139(c)(1), (2) and (3), a qualified disaster means a disaster that results from a terroristic or military action (as defined in section 692(c)(2)), a Presidentially declared disaster (as defined in section 1033(h)(3)), and a disaster that results from an accident involving a common carrier or from any other event which the Secretary determines to be of a catastrophic nature.

August 17, 2006. The excise tax applies irrespective of whether the grant is excludable from the recipient's income as a scholarship or fellowship under section 117.

The IRS and Department of Treasury understand that certain educational grants may have been committed to an individual on or before the date of enactment, the payments of which extend beyond August 17, 2006. Pursuant to this notice, section 4966(c)(1)(A) shall not apply to payments made after August 17, 2006, with respect to an educational grant, if the payment is made pursuant to a grant commitment entered into on or before August 17, 2006. A commitment will be considered entered into on or before August 17, 2006, if:

a. the educational grant was awarded on an objective and nondiscriminatory basis and is reasonable in amount in light of the purposes of the educational grant;

b. the educational grant was not awarded to, nor are payments made pursuant to that grant, to a donor, donor advisor, or any person related to a donor or donor advisor (as described in sections 4967(d) and 4958(f)(7));

c. on or before August 17, 2006: (1) (a) the name of the educational grant recipient, the nature of the educational grant, the amount of the educational grant, the date on which it was awarded, and the educational grant period, were entered on the records of the sponsoring organization or were otherwise adequately evidenced, or (b) notice of the payments to be received was communicated to the payee in writing, and (2) the sponsoring organization keeps a record of such information or notice for a period that ends no earlier than three years after the close of the taxable year in which the last payment is made under the grant; and

d. there is no material change in the amount or in the conditions of the educational grant, such as a required reapplication for the grant.

Notwithstanding the above, section 4967 may apply to any grant that otherwise fits within the criteria specified. Thus, if a sponsoring organization makes an educational grant distribution that results in more than an incidental benefit to a donor, donor advisor, or a person related to a donor or donor advisor, the grant will be subject to excise tax.

Section 6. REQUEST FOR COMMENTS

The IRS and the Department of Treasury request comments regarding this notice and suggestions for future guidance with respect to changes in requirements for donor advised funds and supporting organizations or other changes affecting tax-exempt organizations under the PPA.

Comments should refer to Notice 2006-109 and be submitted by February 1, 2007, to:
    Internal Revenue Service
    SE:T:EO:RA:G (Notice 2006-109)
    P.O. Box 7604
    Ben Franklin Station
    Washington, DC 20044

Submissions may be hand delivered Monday through Friday between the hours of 8a.m. and 4:00 p.m. to:

SE:T:EO:RA:T:G (Notice 2006-109)
Courier's Desk
Internal Revenue Service
1111 Constitution Ave., N.W.
Washington, DC 20224

Alternatively, taxpayers may submit comments electronically to eoppa@irs.gov. Please include "Notice 2006-109" in the subject line of any electronic communications.

All comments will be available for public inspection and copying.

Section 7. PAPERWORK REDUCTION ACT

The collection of information contained in this notice has been reviewed and approved by the Office of Management and Budget in accordance with the Paperwork Reduction Act (44 U.S.C. 3507) under control number 1545-2050. An agency may not conduct or sponsor, and a person is not required to respond to, a collection of information unless the collection of information displays a valid OMB control number.

The requirements to collect information are in Sections 3 and 5 of this notice. Collecting the required information provides private foundations and sponsoring organizations of donor advised funds with relief from excise taxes imposed by sections 4942, 4945 and 4966 of the Code.

The estimated total annual reporting and/or recordkeeping burden is 612,294 hours.

The estimated annual burden per respondent/recordkeeper varies from 7 hours, 53 minutes to 9 hours, 48 minutes, depending on individual circumstances, with an estimated average of 8½ hours. The estimated total number of respondents and/or recordkeepers is 65,000.

The estimated frequency of collection of such information is occasional.

Books or records relating to a collection of information must be retained as long as their contents may become material in the administration of any internal revenue law. Generally, tax returns and tax return information are confidential, as required by 26 U.S.C. section 6103.

Section 8. DRAFTING INFORMATION

The principal authors of this notice are Mary Jo Salins and Robert Fontenrose of the Exempt Organizations, Tax Exempt and Government Entities Division. For further information regarding this notice, contact Ms. Salins at (202) 283-9453, or Mr. Fontenrose at (202) 283-9484 (not a toll-free call).

Appendix E: Notice 2007-21

The text of Notice 2007-21 is found on page 611 of Internal Revenue Bulletin 2007-09 at http://www.irs.gov/pub/irs-irbs/irb07-09.pdf. (Last accessed December 1, 2011.)

Part III - Administrative, Procedural, and Miscellaneous

Study on Donor Advised Funds and Supporting Organizations

Notice 2007-21

PURPOSE

This notice invites public comments in connection with a study being conducted by the Department of the Treasury (the Treasury) and the Internal Revenue Service (the Service) on the organization and operation of donor advised funds (as defined in § 4966(d)(2) of the Internal Revenue Code (Code)) and of supporting organizations described in § 509(a)(3). This study is required by § 1226 of the Pension Protection Act of 2006, Pub. L. No. 109-280, 120 Stat. 780 (2006) (the PPA).

BACKGROUND

Charitable organizations described in § 501(c)(3) are classified under § 509 as either public charities or private foundations, depending on their exempt purposes, the sources of their financial support, or their manner of operation. Private foundations, which typically derive their support from, and are often controlled by, a small number of donors, are subject to a number of anti-abuse rules and excise taxes not applicable to public charities. In addition, contributions to private foundations are subject to lower charitable deduction limits than are contributions to public charities.

Supporting Organizations

Under § 509(a)(3), a supporting organization is a § 501(c)(3) charitable organization that is classified as a public charity, not as a private foundation, as a result of the supporting organization's close relationship to one or more organizations described in §§ 509(a)(1) or 509(a)(2) (referred to in regulations under section 509(a)(3) as "publicly supported organizations"). To qualify as a supporting organization under § 509(a)(3), an organization must satisfy three requirements:
- (A) the organization must be organized and at all times thereafter operated exclusively for the benefit of, to perform the functions of, or to carry out the purposes of one or more specified publicly supported organizations;
- (B) the organization must be operated, supervised, or controlled by or in connection with one or more publicly supported organizations; and
- (C) the organization must not be controlled directly or indirectly by one or more disqualified persons (as defined in § 4946) other than foundation managers and other than one or more publicly supported organizations.

Section 1.509(a)-4 of the Income Tax Regulations provides that the second requirement is met if the supporting organization has one of three relationships with one or more publicly supported organizations. A "Type I" supporting organization is "operated, supervised, or controlled by" a publicly supported organization. This relationship is comparable to that of a parent and subsidiary in that one or more publicly supported organizations can direct the policies, programs or activities of the supporting organization. A "Type II" supporting organization is "supervised or controlled in connection with" one or more publicly supported organizations. In this relationship, the supporting organization and the publicly supported organization(s) are under common supervision or control. A "Type III" supporting organization is "operated in connection with" a publicly supported organization. An organization will qualify as a Type III supporting organization only if it meets certain tests designed to ensure that the organization will be responsive to, and significantly involved in the operations of, the publicly supported organization(s). Under the PPA, this previously informal nomenclature used to describe the relationship between a supporting organization and its publicly supported organizations is incorporated into new §§ 4942(g)(4), 4943(f)(5) and (6), and 4966(d)(4).

Donor Advised Funds

Prior to the PPA, the term donor advised fund was not defined in the Code. However, the term generally was understood to refer to separate funds or accounts established and maintained by public charities to receive contributions from a single donor or a group of donors. The charities had ultimate authority over how the assets in each account were invested and distributed, but the donors, or individuals selected by the donors, were permitted to provide nonbinding recommendations regarding account distributions and/or investments. Donor advised funds often were compared to component funds of certain community trusts. See §§ 1.170A-9(e)(10) and (11).

The PPA adds new § 4966(d)(2), which defines a donor advised fund as a fund or account that is owned and controlled by a sponsoring organization, separately identified by reference to contributions of a donor or donors, and with respect to which the donor or a person appointed or designated by the donor (donor advisor) has or reasonably expects to have advisory privileges with respect to the distribution or investment of the assets in the fund. The term donor advised fund does not include a fund or account (1) that makes distributions only to a single identified organization or governmental entity, or (2) with respect to which a donor advises a sponsoring organization regarding grants for travel, study or similar purposes, provided that certain requirements are met.

A sponsoring organization is defined under new § 4966(d)(1) as a § 170(c) organization that is not a governmental organization (referenced in §§ 170(c)(1) and (2)(A)) or a private foundation and maintains one or more donor advised funds.

Supporting Organizations and Donor Advised Funds as Alternatives to Private Foundations

Traditionally, supporting organizations and donor advised funds have offered donors certain advantages relative to private foundations, such as the possibility of a higher charitable contribution deduction and the avoidance of certain limitations that apply to private foundations, including the § 4941 self-dealing rules, the § 4942 annual payout requirements, and the § 4943 business holdings limits. Although certain advantages remain, new rules enacted as part of the PPA add certain requirements for deductibility of charitable contributions to donor advised funds and impose new restrictions on the operations of donor advised funds and supporting organizations.

New Rules Affecting Supporting Organizations and Donor Advised Funds under the PPA

The PPA contains several provisions intended to improve the accountability of donor advised funds and supporting organizations (see §§ 1226, 1231-1235 and 1241-1245 of the PPA). Those PPA provisions add §§ 4966 and 4967 to the Code, and amend §§ 170, 508, 509, 2055, 2522, 4942, 4943, 4945, 4958, and 6033 of the Code. For a description of some of the new rules, see Notice 2006-109, 2006-51 I.R.B. 1121 (December 18, 2006).

The new rules affecting supporting organizations include: excise taxes on certain payments to a substantial contributor or a related person and on the entire amount of any loan to a disqualified person (§ 4958(c)(3)); the extension of § 4958 to transactions between a supported organization and a person who is a disqualified person of a supporting organization (§ 4958(f)); a grant of regulatory authority to adopt a new payout requirement for certain Type III supporting organizations (PPA § 1241(d)); limits on the permitted business holdings of certain supporting organizations (§ 4943(f)); organizational and operational requirements (§ 509(f)); and reporting requirements (§§ 6033(a)(3)(B) and 6033(l)). In addition, new rules apply to certain private foundations that make grants to certain supporting organizations (§§ 4942(g)(4) and 4945(d)(4)(A)).

The new rules affecting donor advised funds include: definitions of the terms "sponsoring organization" and "donor advised fund" (§ 4966(d)); excise taxes on certain taxable distributions from a donor advised fund (§ 4966(c)); excises taxes on donors, advisors, or related persons who receive certain benefits as a result of a distribution from a donor advised fund (or who advise as to such a distribution) (§ 4967); excise taxes on payments from a donor advised fund to any donor, advisor, or a related person (§§ 4958(c)(2) and 4958(f)(1)(E)); the extension of § 4958 to transactions between the sponsoring organization and certain investment advisors or related persons (§§ 4958(f)(1)(F) and 4958(f)(8)); limits on permitted business holdings (§ 4943(e)); substantiation requirements (§§ 170(f)(18), 2055(e)(5) and 2522(c)(5)); and reporting and disclosure requirements for sponsoring organizations (§§ 508(f) and 6033(k)).

Deductible Charitable Contributions

Generally, an income tax deduction is allowed under § 170 for a charitable contribution made in the year the deduction is claimed, subject to certain limitations and substantiation requirements. See, e.g., U.S. v. American Bar Endowment, 477 U.S. 105 (1986); §§ 1.170A-1(a) and 1.170A-13. Charitable contributions also may be deductible for gift or estate tax purposes. §§ 2522 and 2055. Under the PPA, a taxpayer may deduct a contribution to a donor advised fund only if the sponsoring organization receiving the contribution is one of certain specified types, and the taxpayer making the contribution obtains an acknowledgement from the sponsoring organization that the organization has exclusive legal control over the property contributed. §§ 170(f)(18), 2522(c)(5), and 2055(e)(5).

ISSUES IDENTIFIED FOR FURTHER STUDY UNDER THE PPA

In discussing § 1226 of the PPA, the Technical Explanation prepared by the Joint Committee on Taxation states, in part, "Elsewhere in the bill, provision is made for new rules with respect to donor advised funds and supporting organizations. Many issues arise under current law with respect to such organizations, some of which are addressed in the bill and some of which would benefit from additional study."[101]

Section 1226 of the PPA provides that the Secretary shall undertake a study on the organization and operation of donor advised funds and supporting organizations, and that the study shall specifically consider:

(1) whether the deductions allowed for income, gift, or estate taxes for charitable contributions to sponsoring organizations of donor advised funds or to supporting organizations are appropriate in consideration of (i) the use of contributed assets (including the type, extent, and timing of such use) or (ii) the use of the assets of such organizations for the benefit of the person making the charitable contribution (or a person related to such person),

(2) whether donor advised funds should be required to distribute for charitable purposes a specified amount (whether based on the income or assets of the fund) in order to ensure that the sponsoring organization with respect to the fund is operating consistent with the purposes or functions constituting the basis for its exemption under § 501 or its status as an organization described in § 509(a),

(3) whether the retention by donors to donor advised funds or supporting organizations of rights or privileges with respect to amounts transferred to such organizations (including advisory rights or privileges with respect to the making of grants or the investment of assets) is consistent with the treatment of such transfers as completed gifts that qualify for a deduction for income, gift, or estate taxes, and

(4) whether any of the issues described above also are issues with respect to other forms of charities or charitable donations.

REQUEST FOR PUBLIC COMMENTS

To assist in performing the required study, the Treasury and the Service request comments on the specific issues identified above and other issues relevant to the study. In particular, the Treasury and the Service request comments with respect to the following:

1. What are the advantages and disadvantages of donor advised funds and supporting organizations to the charitable sector, donors, sponsoring organizations, and supported organizations, compared to private foundations and other charitable giving arrangements?

---

[101] Joint Committee on Taxation, *Technical Explanation of H.R. 4, The "Pension Protection Act of 2006," as Passed by the House on July 28, 2006 and as Considered by the Senate on August 3, 2006*, (JCX-38-06), August 3, 2006, at 333.

2. How should the amount and availability of a charitable contribution deduction for a transfer of assets to a donor advised fund or a supporting organization, and the tax-exempt status or foundation classification of the donee, be determined if:
   a. the transferred assets are paid to, or used for the benefit of, the donor or persons related to the donor (including, for example, salaries and other compensation arrangements, loans, or any other personal benefits or rights)?
   b. the donor has investment control over the transferred assets?
   c. there is an expectation that the donor's "advice" will be followed, or will be the sole or primary consideration, in determining distributions from, or investment of the assets in, the supporting organization or the donor advised fund?
   d. the donor or the donee has option rights (e.g., puts, calls, or rights of first refusal) with respect to the transferred assets?
   e. the transferred assets are appreciated real, personal, or intangible property that is not readily convertible to cash?
3. What are the effects or the expected effects of the PPA provisions (including the § 4958 excess benefit transaction tax amendments applicable to donor advised funds and supporting organizations) on the practices and behavior of donors, donor advised funds, sponsoring organizations, supporting organizations and supported organizations?
4. What would be appropriate payout requirements, and why, for:
   a. donor advised funds?
   b. funds that are excepted from donor advised fund treatment by statute or by the authority of the Secretary, but for which the donor retains meaningful rights with respect to the investment or use of the transferred amounts?
   c. supporting organizations?
   d. any other types of charities?
5. What are the advantages and disadvantages of perpetual existence of donor advised funds or supporting organizations?
6. What other types of charitable giving arrangements give rise to any of the above issues?

Section 1226 of the PPA provides that, not later than August 16, 2007, the Secretary shall submit to the Congress a report on the study. Comments should refer to Notice 2007-21 and be submitted by April 9, 2007, to:
Internal Revenue Service
P.O. Box 7604
Ben Franklin Station
Washington, D.C. 20044
Attn: CC:PA:LPD:PR
Room 5203
Alternatively, comments may be submitted electronically via e-mail to Notice.Comments@irscounsel.treas.gov. The comments you submit will be available for public inspection and copying.

DRAFTING INFORMATION

The principal authors of this notice are Robert Fontenrose of the Exempt Organizations, Tax Exempt and Government Entities Division, and Susan J. Kassell of the Office of Associate Chief

Counsel (Income Tax & Accounting). For further information regarding exempt organization issues contact Mr. Fontenrose at (202) 283-9484 (not a toll-free call). For further information regarding charitable contribution issues, contact Ms. Kassell at (202) 622-5020 (not a toll-free call).

www.ingramcontent.com/pod-product-compliance
Lightning Source LLC
Chambersburg PA
CBHW081221280526
45787CB00006B/2477